THE
KEYS
TO
CREATIVITY

THE
KEYS
TO
CREATIVITY

Gary Bertwistle

About *The Keys to Creativity*

Ideas, imagination and creative thinking are increasingly becoming sought-after qualities and important points of difference in today's society. No matter what stage of life you are at or how creative you may be, you can always learn to make better use of your creative ability.

Everyone is born with a natural creative talent and a wonderful imagination that enables them to be creative and generate great ideas. The secret lies in knowing how to tap into that natural ability in order to unlock these ideas and reach your full creative potential.

The Keys to Creativity will encourage you to challenge the thinking that has conditioned you as an adult, and to remove the barriers that are currently holding you back from achieving your goals. This book will give you unique breakthrough tools and techniques to help you develop better ideas and more of them in all areas of your life, as well as a new, unquestionable belief in the creative ability you already possess!

First published in 2006 by
Blue Moon Publishing
Building 14, The Entertainment Quarter
Driver Avenue
Moore Park NSW 1363

Revised edition.

National Library of Australia Cataloguing-in-Publication data:

      Bertwistle, Gary.

      The keys to creativity.

      Includes index.

      ISBN 0 646 45618 0.

      1. Creative ability in business. 2. Creative ability -

      Psychological aspects. I. Title.

      650.1

Cover design by Inqbase.

Editing and layout by Michael Hanrahan (www.mhps.com.au).

Printed in Australia by McPherson's Printing.

CONTENTS

To my wife Emanda, thank you for your support and dedication and for making sense of all my rambling ...

INTRODUCTION

I am not a university professor, nor am I an ex–creative director of a big ad agency, or even a certified psychologist; I am just a normal guy who has a passion for ideas and who believes he has something valuable to share with others.

My first foray into the workforce was in a department store despatch, unloading trucks and sweeping floors. I worked my way through department store management, worked on the road managing rock bands, ran the marketing and promotions campaigns for large shopping centres, and finally commenced an eight-year stint in promotions and marketing for radio stations. In 1997, I left the radio industry altogether to set up my own company — Blue Moon Creative — to teach others about creativity and what we can do to think differently.

No matter what occupation I had, I was always considered to be an ideas person, as creativity is something

I have always been passionate about. I care very much about the process of idea generation, and I am constantly searching for ways of doing it better. I have read a lot of books about creativity over the years. Some of these books were very good (and I have listed a few at the back of this book for your reference[1]), while others I think missed their mark. The more I read, the more convinced I became that there is a need for a real-world approach to creativity.

This book is not about making you creative, as nobody can *make* you creative; they can only help you to make better use of the creativity that you already have inside. Indeed, this book is all about giving you practical tips and tools to better harness that creative ability and put it to use. Many — in fact most — books on the topic of creativity seem to espouse a great deal of theory, which is fine in the theory-based world of academia, but when it comes to the crunch they don't necessarily assist you to generate great ideas in the real world. I feel it is important to have a selection of tools available at your fingertips that you can use in real-life situations. The processes and tools in this book have been road-tested in workshops and proven through my own experiences, so I know they really do work. They are the 'keys' to your creative potential, and they work out there on the street, where your ideas make you the person you are, separate you from the next person, and distinguish your company from its competition.

Some of the tools or keys in this book you may already have at your disposal, while others you may not

---

1   Appendix A: Gary's recommended book list.

have seen or used before. I hope they may be of value to you in the near future. Not every concept in this book will feel comfortable to you, so I have endeavoured to give you a variety of tools to allow you the flexibility to find the ones that feel 'right' for you. There are ideas that you can use when you are generating ideas on your own, and some that you can use to leverage ideas with and from a group. Others you will be able to use in either situation.

We all have natural creative talent lying within us that is just waiting to be unlocked. My purpose in writing this book is to help you to make use of that creative potential and help you to be the best that you can be. I hope that after reading *The Keys to Creativity* you will walk away with a strong and unquestionable belief in your own creative ability, and that you will have the necessary tools and techniques on hand to develop better ideas and more of them. From this strong foundation, I hope to encourage you to use your creativity on a daily basis and to foster the same in others around you. In this world of growing uniformity of ideas and actions, I hope you will increasingly want to stand out from the crowd and to always be alert to the possibility of new and alternative ways of doing things.

Thank you for investing your valuable time to read this book. There are so many books to choose from at any given time; I appreciate your faith in mine and I feel privileged that you have chosen to read this one.

Gary Bertwistle
Sydney, 2006

1 THE BASICS

GET SET

There are a couple of things that I would like to recommend to you just before we get started …

As you explore the ideas in this book, you will no doubt come across snippets of information, useful points, as well as tips and tools that you particularly wish to remember. I have always found it valuable to keep a pencil and coloured highlighter pen within easy reach when reading, so that as I move through a book I can highlight any points that are interesting and perhaps also jot down any notes or action points as I go. If you do highlight interesting phrases, quotes, tips and tools as you read a book, I would like to suggest that you come back to the book a week or so after completing it and copy the highlighted pieces into a journal kept especially for this purpose. By transferring the key points that you have taken from the book into your journal, not only are you reviewing your notes and enhancing your learning, your journal also becomes a summary of all the books that you have read and develops into a valuable source of book summaries and reference material for future use. Feel free to make this information as interesting as you wish — use colour, draw maps and pictures, whatever makes it interesting and fun for you. A large percentage of the world's population are visual learners, and the use of colour is thought to greatly Increase learning and memory retention, so why not give it a try and see if it works for you? By highlighting and note-taking as you read the book, this valuable summary process will only take a few additional minutes of your time once you have completed the book.

If at all possible I would also recommend finding a relaxing spot to read, whether that may be in the shade outside under a tree, by the water, curled up on the lounge, or nestled back in the seat of a Boeing 747 en route to your next travel destination. You may wish to just breathe in the fresh air for a few moments, play some soothing music in the background, or perhaps even light some incense or aromatic oils to encourage you to slow down, kick back and relax. You will find that you will be much more open to new ideas, and you will draw much greater benefit from your reading in this relaxed state. As I write this passage, I am sitting at home, windows wide open, vanilla incense burning, and I have some peaceful Native American music playing in the background. For me, this is perfect — it is relaxing whilst still allowing me to concentrate and create. However, this set-up may not work for you, so create your own relaxed environment where you feel comfortable, then sit back and prepare to consider the keys to creativity that this book presents!

So what is creativity?

If I asked you to give yourself a score from one to ten as to how creative you are, what would your answer be? If I were to then ask you to give yourself a score between one and ten as to your ability to come up with ideas or solutions for an issue, event or question, what would your answer be? Make sure you give yourself a score before reading on, even if you just think about it without writing it down.

How different were your answers? In workshops I find that people tend to give very different answers to these two questions. The average score for individuals rating their creativity is anywhere between three and five, yet those same individuals generally rate their ability to generate ideas as more like seven to nine. Why is that? Well there are a number of reasons, mostly centred on people's perceptions, belief structures and how they choose to define creativity.

Firstly, let's define creativity. Is it an ability to look at things differently? Is it coming up with a new idea? Is it innovating, looking outside the square, challenging the way things are currently done, or is it art, a new thought, or just not being afraid to try new things? Perhaps it is having fun, expressing yourself and being weird? Some people define creativity as the process of creating something tangible; that is, to be creative you must have the idea *and* be able to do it. They believe that having an idea does *not necessarily* mean that it can be done … it's just an idea. Can you have an idea without being creative? Or, can you be creative without having an idea? Most people would say they are one and the same thing.

My own definition of creativity is having an ability to look at things differently. I believe creativity is creating something that was not there before, whether this be a solution to a problem or a new piece of computer software. Creativity can also be adapting an existing idea to make it different, by changing, improving or enhancing it, such as inventing a new ice cream flavour.

Think about the following scenarios and ask yourself once again if you are creative: Have you ever dressed up in a fancy dress costume for a party? Have you ever been imaginative throwing a party of your own? How about when you designed the layout of your office, your bedroom or your lounge room at home; did that not require you to be creative? What about that amazing present you once bought for your friend and she asked how you ever thought of it. These are all situations where you used your creative mind in one way or another. You may find that you tend to use your creativity more often in a social environment, possibly feeling less comfortable using it in a work environment, but that does not make it any less valuable or mean that you are not creative.

Creativity may really be as simple as having a new idea, coming up with a solution to a complex problem from a completely different angle, or even just trying something new. What's your new definition of creativity? Have fun with it and give it your own angle. Forget what everyone else thinks it is, and give it your own spin. I encourage people to think in terms of *options*. In what ways could you develop more than one *option* to solve this problem? You can't find *options* or ways of doing things without being creative, and the more options you push for the more you exercise your creativity. So if the term *creativity* bothers you, or you see creativity as having to come up with something unique and earth-shattering, then think of it differently. Think of it as coming up with *options*. Consider yourself a freethinker — a person who is free to think differently and who can come up with lots of options. By defining creativity in this way, does it not make you think that perhaps there isn't as much to this creativity hype as you originally thought? *Now* how would you score yourself?

Perception

Now, back to that question I asked you at the beginning of the chapter about rating your creativity out of ten. Did you rate your creativity based on your perception of other people's creativity? Say, for example, there is a guy in your office whom you regard as really creative and you rate him as an eight or nine as far as creativity is concerned. In comparison to him, do you feel you must be more like a five, because you believe you are a lot less creative than he is? We are generally quite hard on ourselves when asked to score our own creativity, particularly when we compare ourselves to others. This in itself can become a limiting belief. Most people are surprised to learn that the person they were comparing themselves to invariably scores their creativity higher than they did their own.

If individuals could only overcome false beliefs about their creative talents they would often look behind themselves and discover a trail of creativity that others would only marvel at. In workshops I often hear people saying that they are 'terrible at creativity', yet someone else in the group, often a work associate, will argue that they think this person is excellent at coming up with ideas and is really creative. The individual generally finds this to be quite a confronting experience, and it is only when presented with evidence of their creativity in front of the group that they acknowledge that others may perceive them as being creative. They often need to overcome years of self-talk before they can start to think, 'Hey, maybe they are right and I *am* creative …'

One such person was Jan, the wife of a friend of mine. Peter and Jan, an artist, were visiting my workshop venue in Sydney called The Vault one Saturday afternoon. Peter had told Jan all about the workshop space as he thought she might be interested in looking at the room from an artistic point of view, and they popped by to check it out. During the course of conversation we also discussed Jan's work, and I expressed an interest in seeing some of it at a later date. I was delighted when Jan dropped in a few weeks later with some of her artwork to show me. I have to say I was really bowled over with the quality — it was quite amazing. As she was leaving that day, I made a comment about how great it was to meet someone as creative as she was. What Jan said next stunned me completely. She turned to me and innocently said, 'Oh I am not creative!'

This reply of course intrigued me, and I had to ask her more about it and why she didn't consider herself creative. 'Oh no, I just do what I really enjoy doing, I just paint what I see,' Jan said. 'People who do pottery and sculpture, they are really creative ones, I am just doing what I enjoy doing.' This response made me even more fascinated about the subject of creative thinking, and in particular people's perception of their own creativity. At this point I have to mention that just eight weeks after this conversation, Jan won one of the most prestigious art awards in Australia and was interviewed on every major television and radio station in the country. Twelve months further down the track and Jan has just won the same prestigious art award for the second year running … oh to be that uncreative!

Consider the following poem …

IF – by Rudyard Kipling

If you can keep your head when all about you

Are losing theirs and blaming it on you;

If you can trust yourself when all men doubt you,

But make allowance for their doubting too;

If you can wait and not be tired by waiting

Or, being lied about, don't deal in lies,

Or, being hated, don't give way to hating,

And yet don't look too good, nor talk too wise;

If you can dream – and not make your dreams your master;

If you can think – and not make thoughts your aim;

If you can meet with triumph and disaster

And treat those two imposters just the same;

If you can bear to hear the truth you've spoken

Twisted by knaves to make a trap for fools,

Or watch the things you gave your life to broken,

And stoop and build 'em up with worn-out tools;

If you can make one heap of all your winnings

And risk it on one turn of pitch-and-toss,

And lose, and start again at your beginnings

And never breathe a word about your loss;

If you can force your heart and nerve and sinew

To serve your turn long after they are gone,

And so hold on when there is nothing in you

Except the will which says to them: 'hold on';

If you can talk with crowds and keep your virtue,

Or walk with kings – nor lose the common touch;

If neither foes nor loving friends can hurt you;

If all men count with you, but none too much;

If you can fill the unforgiving minute

With sixty seconds' worth of distance run –

Yours is the Earth and everything that's in it,

And – which is more – you'll be a man my son!

The moral of the story is to not let your perception of other people's creativity influence what and how you think about your own creative ability. Jan truly did not believe that she was creative — by her definition it was potters and sculptures who truly were creative, yet to someone like me her talent was self-evident. No-one, including yourself, knows what you are capable of. We are just starting to discover the true potential of the human mind, so don't let yourself or anyone else put a limit on your creative ability and what you are capable of. Don't fear what others think — if it feels right and you've thought it out, go for it, speak up. Indeed, there are only two things we know for certain about the human brain — the first is that it is unknown, and the second is that it's underestimated. Don't underestimate yourself and your abilities!

'Our deepest fear is not that we are inadequate.
Our deepest fear is that we are powerful beyond measure.'[2]

---

2   Marianne Williamson, from *A Return to Love: Reflections on the Principles of a Course in Miracles*, Harper Collins, 1992. From chapter 7, section 3.

YOUR BELIEF STRUCTURE

Next I wish to move on to discussing how your belief structure can impact on your creativity. If you gave yourself a score of six in the creativity question earlier in the chapter and believe that you can do better, then you are off to a good start in your quest for improving your creativity. If, however, you gave yourself a score of six and truly believe that you are only capable of a six, then you are creating a limiting belief about your capabilities that can hold you back from achieving your creative potential.

I repeatedly hear people say, 'Oh I am not creative,' or, 'I don't have a creative bone in my body,' or, 'No, my sister is the creative one in our family.' Guess what — if you constantly repeat this sort of dialogue to yourself and to others, your brain then searches for evidence that this is in fact so. The brain has a hard time distinguishing between what is imaginary and what is real, and when you repeatedly say, 'I am not creative,' you are literally programming yourself not to be creative and not to be able to come up with ideas! You may be surprised to learn that the average person has around 20,000 words of 'self-talk' every day. If these words are negative and reinforce what you believe you can't do and what you believe you are not capable of, then they will become a self-fulfilling prophecy. From a young age, many people are subconsciously telling themselves that they cannot do things or that they are 'not' something. From this moment forward, make a conscious choice not to let yourself be one of these people. Don't let that self-talk stop you from achieving what you want to achieve.

Even successful people can let self-talk and their beliefs get in the way of their creative potential. These are people who do not believe they are creative because they are naturally talented and they do it without conscious thought or without trying very hard. I know of many successful artists and writers who do not consider themselves creative because they haven't struggled as others do.

Let's take Jan as an example once again. Jan doesn't believe she is creative; she says she just enjoys what she does, and it is others such as sculptors (whose work she regards as more difficult than painting) who are creative. Views such as these effectively place limiting beliefs on those who hold them. Often these people also end up believing they are only talented in one particular area — the one book they wrote that was incredibly successful or the song that sold a million copies. They may not believe they can repeat the success or that they can be creative in other areas of their life.

Once you believe in your ability to generate ideas, your first step should be to control the voice inside of you — reprogram it to say positive things about your creativity. That little voice inside your head and the language you use to talk to others must reinforce the fact that you believe you are creative. Of course there will be times when you stumble, when people will reject an idea that you have had or when an idea doesn't come to you immediately. Not every one of your ideas will be a good one, not all of them will work, and many will be totally impractical, but that is fine because you should know that you have thousands of ideas all the time, and with some more practice and the right tools, you will continue to be better than you currently are.

I am not suggesting that you stand in front of the mirror each morning and say to yourself, 'I am creative, I am an ideas person,' although you can do it that way if you feel so inclined. What I am suggesting is that when you have the opportunity to approach something differently or to solve a problem, you just quietly say to yourself, 'I can do this. I know I can find a different way to do this. I have just as much ability as the next person, and I am going to be the one to do it,' or something of that nature. You can develop your own dialogue to suit yourself. I generally say to myself, 'I can do this, I can do this,' and once I have set myself up and I have a positive mental framework in place, I then set about using the tools that follow in this book to develop my ideas. Another one of my self-programming favourites is to change 'can't' into 'what else?' If you ask this question consistently, you will find you are on your way to creating still more options. It is important to really believe in your creativity and to ensure that your self-talk carries conviction. You don't need to be yelling out for all to hear (although you may choose to do that), you just have to say it and believe it … with passion!

The brain can't hold two contrary thoughts at once. Your brain will either believe you are not creative or you are creative, depending on what you tell it, and it will decide based on the voice that rings loudest in your own mind. I was once on a plane returning from a trip to London, and when the in-flight movie had finished, some music clips were played. There was a clip of the rock band U2 playing live at Slane Castle in Ireland. The lead singer of the band, Bono, was being interviewed back-stage. He said, 'Going on stage each night is like being a fighter and going into the ring; except your opponent is yourself, and you just hope on the night, your best side wins.' This illustrates the concept of your brain not being able to hold two contrary thoughts at once. You just hope the right side of your brain — the side that does believe in your creativity — wins on the night.

There is a story of a man who went to visit a Buddhist monk, looking to learn the secret of Zen. He approached the monk and said, 'Master, what is the secret of Zen?' The Master looked at the man and quietly said, 'When working, just work, when eating, just eat and when rest-ing, just rest.' The Master then looked away. Of course the man was perplexed by the simplicity of the answer, and said, 'Surely that can't be it?' The Master looked at the man and replied, 'It is, and it's surprising how few people can do it.'

Self-programming really is a simple yet crucial step to developing your creative talent, but so few people actually do it. Start today to change the words you say to yourself and others, and experience the positive out-comes it can have on the way you look at your abilities and your place in the world.

Whole-Brain Thinking and Why It Is Important

I would love it if I was paid a dollar every time someone walked up to me at a workshop and asked me whether I really believe that anyone can learn to be *more* creative. While it is true that the environment you grew up in and the one you now work in can and do greatly affect the way you perceive and use your creativity, the good news is that creativity and whole-brain thinking are learned processes, and everyone can learn new techniques that will enable them to develop more and better ideas. We are all born with the hardware to be creative, and no matter what stage of life you are at or how creative you may think you are currently, you can learn to make better use of your creative ability based on what you have inside you right at this minute. Just hearing people say the words *more* and *better use* is the first step, because they are acknowledging that there is something there to begin with ... and there is!

Your brain and how it works

Now, I don't profess to be a medical expert by any stretch of the imagination, but at this point I would like to touch briefly on the physical structure of the brain to explain how it works, where your creativity comes from, and how to get the most from it. If you read textbooks on thinking, creativity and the brain, you will discover that there are essentially three distinct areas of the human brain. These parts are known as the reptilian, the mammalian and the thinking brain. The reptilian brain is at the base of your skull, and it controls all of your basic functions and instincts such as breathing and heart rate. The centre part of your brain which wraps around the brain stem is the mammalian brain; this controls all of your emotions. If you make a fist with one hand and wrap the other hand over the top of this fist, the wrist of your first hand represents your reptilian brain, the fist represents your mammalian brain, and the hand that wraps over your fist is your thinking brain. The thinking part of the brain is what I am particularly concerned with here — it is the part of the brain that handles all of our intelligence and that makes us most human, and unique as a species. It handles seeing, hearing, creating, thinking, talking; all the higher intelligences. This is where all your decisions are made, where you organise your world, where your experiences are stored, where your speech is produced, and so on. It contains everything you'll ever need to learn about anything at any time.

Now this 'thinking' part of the brain is split into two — the left and right brain. The left brain specialises in logic and analysis, dealing with academic-type functions such as language and mathematical processes. The right part of the brain is concerned with creative functions such as rhyme, music, visual impressions, colour and pictures. It's your dreaming side and the imaginative side of the brain. We are all born with both the left and right parts of our brains, so we are all born with the ability to create, dream and use our imagination, as well as to be analytical and logical.

Why then do we tend to become so locked in to using the left side of the brain in preference to using our creative right side? One theory is that as we grow and develop, we begin to build barriers between our left and right brains. As we get older we rely more and more on the left side of our brains, as this is the side that we are encouraged to use. Think about it — when you are a child you don't know what to do and what not to do, what is right and what is wrong. You aren't aware of what things can't be done so you just do things — you explore, and you ask the question 'why not?' You put your hands where they are not supposed to be put, and you put things in your hands and your mouth that aren't supposed to go there because you don't know any different. As a child, you are constantly challenging things and trying new things because that is part of growing up. As we grow up we are increasingly encouraged not to daydream, not to think too differently, not to touch things, not to try things, not to scribble or doodle, and we start to learn rules, decide what is right or wrong, look at those around us, and develop beliefs about our own lives. It is when we start forming these beliefs and rules that we start to build the barriers that stop us from trying new things and innovating, and we increasingly tend to live in a safe or known world. In fact, we even begin teaching ourselves how to be *uncreative*, how *not* to be innovative, and how *not* to challenge things because we prefer to exist in our comfort zone.

Research conducted in the USA has suggested that if we arbitrarily allocate to a two-year-old child a 100%

ability to look at things differently (to be creative, to use their imagination, to think about things differently), by the time they are five years old their ability to look at things differently, to use their imagination and to create has shrunk to 40% of what it was. By the time they are aged forty, that creative ability has dropped to 2%. Isn't it scary to think that between the ages of two and forty we lose 98% of our innate ability to create, to dream, to use our imagination?

The important thing to remember is that although this research concluded we generally use only 2% of our potential, by age forty the other 98% is not lost, it is just not being used. The purpose of this book is to enable you to unlock that other 98%.

As adults, when we come across opportunities as well as challenges, we find ourselves approaching them in the same way and habitually ignoring the more creative solutions from the right side of the brain, due to time constraints, lack of belief in our ability and all the other logical reasons we have come up with over the years. In reality, neither solely left-brain or right-brain thinking is to be preferred in the generation of ideas and creativity; it is whole-brain thinking that we should be striving for. Whole-brain thinking is all about having access to both sides of the thinking mind, to give us more options and therefore the opportunity for more and better ideas. Ideally we want to be able to think analytically when required without being ruled by logic. Logic is an important part of every creative process; we just can't let it hinder our imagination in the early part of idea generation.

I have been very fortunate in that I was brought up in creative surroundings that encouraged the use of my right brain as well as my left brain (that is, whole-brain thinking). When I was younger, both my mother and grandmother, 'nanna', were interested and involved in arts and crafts. They would do macramé, origami and flower arranging. My nanna would even produce artwork using different bark from trees, dried flowers and grasses, using chalk to colour the bark and make it into wonderful pieces of art to frame and hang on the walls. Although I was very young at the time, I can distinctly remember how good they both were at all the creative arts they took up. Now I do not profess an intense interest in the arts, but I do believe that those early days certainly ignited and fostered the creative side of my mind. I even remember sitting in front of the television on a Sunday afternoon, coloured paper at the ready, riveted to a particular television show demonstrating how to do origami. Of course my swan looked more like a ball of knitting yarn than anything resembling an elegant bird, but this did form an important early stage of my creative journey!

My dad, in contrast, was a bank manager all of his working life, and he was very logical and analytical in his approach to business and life. At work, he regularly made important decisions regarding loans and deals worth millions of dollars. So, while my mother and nanna stimulated my creative side, the left side of my mind was also stimulated by my dad's analytical and logical thinking. Thankfully, I was fortunate enough to have had the best of both worlds — an environment that stimulated a fertile imagination, while still fostering the ability to think logically when required.

Now you might be thinking, 'That's all great, but what if you did not have a creative upbringing or influence … what now?' The important thing to remember is that although you may not be actively using your creative ability a great deal as an adult, you have not lost any of the creative ability or imagination that you had as a child; it's just a matter of getting to it. That is the challenge. I liken it to drilling for oil — we know the oil is down there; it is a matter of drilling through the surface and getting down to it. The same applies to creativity. Once we know creativity is there just below the surface, we can work on removing the barriers in order to give us access to the wealth of ideas that are waiting.

You have probably heard the phrase 'thinking outside the box'. Well, here is a thought from best-selling author and personal coach Anthony Robbins:

> 'We live in a box, eat breakfast from a box, go to work
> in a box, work in a box, then we go home and watch
> the box (some even have dinner from a box!).'[3]

Is it any wonder that we need to 'think outside the box'? This book is going to bend, disfigure, move, change and even remove the box to allow you to explore your creative potential. Some of the suggestions in this book will seem too easy, too basic, like … that's it? Remember that

---

3   Anthony Robbins, *Personal Power* audio program.

quite often the secret lies in the easy stuff, the simple things we can do to start the freethinking juices flowing, the simple things that we tend to forget or fail to find the time for. Just because it is simple does not mean it is not valuable. This book is all about removing the barriers that keep you within the box and getting you to think differently.

WHY IS CREATIVITY IMPORTANT?

Why is it that we want to enhance our creativity in today's world? Creativity is that intangible 'something' that separates us as an individual from those around us, and it is truly our most powerful asset. It contributes to our ability to solve problems, to challenge ourselves, and to find ways to have a more successful and enjoyable life. Creativity makes life interesting; it brings us joy and sometimes even pain. But above all else, creativity keeps us moving forward as an individual, and as a culture.

The creation of new ideas is the foundation of all human progress. Our imagination develops the pictures of our future; it helps to construct our dreams, and finds the ways to make those dreams come to life. One of the world's great creative minds, Albert Einstein, said many years ago, 'Imagination is more important than knowledge.' The quality of our future will depend on our ability to problem-solve and find solutions to the daily issues that confront us. Those who can create and innovate will lead the generations to come.

In years past, better knowledge in business gave individuals, corporations and even countries the edge over their competition. More recently that edge has also been gained through the use of technology. However, with technology and people's access to technology progressing at such a rapid rate and with knowledge doubling almost yearly, it is increasingly becoming less of a point of difference. Now when news breaks or a new method or technology emerges, it can be around the world in seconds. (No sooner have you bought a new mobile phone than your best friend shows you the newly released model with camera and automatic hand massager. Yours is only six weeks old, and it's already out of date!) Ideas, imagination and creative thinking are increasingly becoming the important points of difference and the most sought-after qualities that you and those around you can have in today's society. What's more, your creativity is one of the only things that cannot be copied. It makes you unique. It's what makes you special.

There's a saying: 'If you always do what you've always done, you always get what you've always got.' Mediocrity is all around us. Think about the possibility that perhaps in the future what you've currently got will not be good enough, and that if you keep doing what you are currently doing then chances are that in the future you just won't cut it and you will be left behind in this increasingly competitive world.

Perhaps a better saying for us to stick on our walls is this:

If you do today what you did yesterday, you'll be beaten.

*If you do today what others are doing now,
you'll be competitive.*

*To win, you must seek to do today what
others will be doing tomorrow.*

Break out of the everyday and put your creative mind to use! What a waste it is to not make use of the gift of creativity in whatever form you wish to use it, whether that may be to get ahead in business or start that sculpting that you have always wanted to do, or the garden you have always wanted to create, or the music you have always wanted to be able to play. Don't die with the music in you; give it the opportunity to shine through, and make yourself a better, happier and more balanced person. Too often we only really think when confronted with a problem, and we very rarely take the time to proactively think about ideas, to think about new ways to do something, or to consider the potential 'what ifs'. I hope this book gives you some simple but effective approaches to ignite your fire, to stimulate your creative freethinking juices, and to remove those barriers that are holding you back from achieving your creative potential.

2 REMOVING THE BARRIERS TO CREATIVITY

As I mentioned in the previous chapter, everyone has their own barriers to creativity, those things that prevent them from moving beyond their comfort zone and trying new things. In the first part of this chapter we are going to identify the key barriers to creativity and how to remove them, and then move on to identifying practices that can help you to foster creativity in your world.

BELIEVE IT AND YOU WILL SEE IT

Not having a strong belief in our own creative ability is possibly the most significant barrier to finding and utilising our creative potential. I am constantly surprised by the number of inordinately creative people who believe that they need to go to others for good ideas or to have their problems solved. What a waste of talent!

I left the radio industry in 1997 to open Blue Moon Creative, and since then I have worked with a very broad cross-section of companies on creativity and the process of idea generation. I have found that certain people in every organisation (whether that organisation is an advertising agency or a potato grower) tend to be seen as the 'creatives' within the company. These people are seen to be responsible for coming up with the ideas and creative solutions within the organisation, and everyone else — whether they be the 'suits', the administrative staff or the sales people — seems to abdicate all creativity to them. Others turn to them for ideas rather than utilising their own creativity. Take advertising agencies as a perfect example. Within any advertising agency there is a group of people, in this example even called the 'creatives', whose sole job it is to design great ideas for their company and the company's clients. Meanwhile, there is a whole office full of executives and administrators sitting in the same space, just brimming with ideas, who do not have the opportunity to be heard. Wouldn't it be great both for the companies involved and for their staff if they all had the belief and the opportunity to express their ideas in the workplace? What a wealth of ideas to tap into!

I've been fortunate to work with some incredibly talented and creative people over the years, and I have found the common trait these 'creative' people possess is a conviction in their ability to come up with ideas and to find many and varied solutions to all sorts of challenges, combined with the opportunity for constant practice. Characteristically these creative types have a strong belief in their own ability to generate ideas, they are often not satisfied with the status quo, and they feel very comfortable approaching issues and challenges in a unique manner. They also recognise that there is no such thing as just being creative; it is something they work at constantly. These people are also 'what else' people. They are not satisfied with the status quo, and their internal dialogue is always asking 'what else?' These people live in a land of possibilities. I have often had a group of creative directors from large advertising agencies attend workshops with me simply because they want to be more creative than they already are.

In contrast, I have noticed that many people, rather than embracing any suggestion that they may be creative, often shy away from being labelled as such. They feel that to say they are creative puts a certain amount of pressure and responsibility on them, and they fear an expectation may develop which will see them pressured to come up with unbelievably outstanding ideas on a regular basis. Let go of that pressure! Rather, think about the reality that you are an ideas person and that you can come up with many and varied ideas and solutions to problems on a regular basis. The important thing to remember is that we all have a choice as to how much and how often we use our creativity.

Don't use barriers such as belief and fear as excuses not to look for different and better ways of doing things. Realise that creative ability and creative behaviour are two separate things. Just because you have not fully utilised your creativity doesn't mean that it isn't there. Refuse to believe the ridiculous notion that you are not creative because you can't recall anything that you have done recently that you would regard as creative. You are probably using your creative talents in many small ways every day and are completely unaware of it on a conscious level. Ordinary people are having great ideas every day and using them to solve problems, find solutions and excel in their chosen jobs; they just don't consider that it is creativity they are using or give themselves the credit they deserve. Believe in that ability and you will go far!

Although I did not know it at the time, when I was in my final years of high school I met the first of many mentors who instilled in me a belief in my own ability to achieve and succeed. I was an average runner at high school, and I would go to the school athletics carnival for a number of reasons, none of which had anything to do with running — it was a day out of the classroom, it was a chance to impress the girls, and everybody else went. The only running training I had done to this point was rather by accident than design. I had a sunset curfew as a kid — my mum insisted that I be home from playing touch football with friends by the time the sun went down. Naturally I would always stay out for far too long, and so three or four times a week I was in a mad panic to run the five kilometres home along the streets of Brisbane to make it back in time. Needless to say, my fitness always improved over summer!

This particular year I entered the school cross-country championships, and to my own immense surprise I won it with ease. I literally could not believe that I could win a race, let alone a cross-country. In fact I was so dumbfounded that I won that I thought I must have missed some of the course! There was someone, however, who had noticed my fairly impressive performance (without structured training of any sort that he knew about) — a physical education teacher from school called Vince Hopgood.

Vince was a young guy in his mid twenties, and after the cross-country event he approached me to talk about running and the potential I had shown. He said he believed that I had a lot of natural ability and with the right instruction could be a fine runner, which was a complete shock to me! Vince began training me, and each day he would applaud the good work I did and encourage me when I slacked off, and he constantly had me focus on what had to be done and the fact that I *could* do it! To this day I remember the difference that Vince made, not only to my belief structure in a running sense but also towards my life in general. Here was a guy who really wanted to help young people achieve and be the best that they could be, and he wanted me to know that I had ability but that the rest was up to me. Vince and I trained together that season, and I ended up winning the school middle distance championships and was a member of the team that won the Queensland cross-country championships the following year.

We all need to have people around us who will challenge us, stimulate us, encourage us, and most of all bring out the best in us. I hope that you have been fortunate enough to have had a Vince or someone like him in your life at some point; someone who sees what we either can't see or won't see in ourselves. Look around you, and strive to have people around you whom you respect and who will challenge and stimulate you. Occasionally you may find yourself surrounded by a group who will hijack your creative juices by constantly knocking your ideas or criticising what you do and say, and by providing less than complimentary comments when presented with new or different ways of doing something. Try to make sure wherever possible that you are surrounded by as many positive, creative people as possible who will encourage you and contribute to the creative environment you are designing for yourself. With this support, we learn to develop positive self-talk, a belief that we are creative and that we have the qualities of a creative person. In fact, we should encourage not only ourselves, but also those we work with, live with and share our lives with to break out, to try new things and to have the confidence to think differently.

You may have seen the road movie *Thelma & Louise*, about two women on the run from the law. At one point early in the movie, Louise says to Thelma, 'You get what you settle for.' This has such resonance for me. If you believe that you are not creative, then that is exactly what you're going to have to settle for. On the other hand, if you have a strong abiding belief in your ability to think differently and to come up with creative solutions to problems and challenges then I think you will begin to reflect that belief. Belief plays such an important role — don't settle for anything less than your best. Raise the bar on your ideas, your belief in your ideas and your commitment to challenge the way things are done.

In fact, if you allow me to continue for a moment the athletic theme that we began earlier, I think you would agree that athletes at an elite level display an extraordinary degree of belief in their ability, some would say even to the extent of arrogance. Do you really think that there are any extraordinary athletes out there who get to where they are without a strong belief in their ability? How can you be the fastest in the world in your distance if you do not believe you can be the fastest? I remember talking to world champion English athlete Roger Black. Roger won the silver medal in the men's 400 metres at the 1996 Atlanta Olympic Games, and is an incredible talent. He said that when he spoke to other great sportspeople about their ability to compete, he discovered that the ones who were the best, the ones who really stood out, were the ones who *needed* to win. They did not just *want* to win, they *needed* to win, they *needed* it more than the others.

Exercising your creativity

The other thing these athletes do which replicates other successfully creative people is that they practice. It is really important to remember that if you wish to develop your creativity then it needs to be exercised constantly. In much the same fashion as a sports person goes to the gym to work out and grow muscles, you have to exercise day after day in order to become creatively fit. What I am talking about here is using the right and left sides of your brain on a regular basis, so that you have access to both the analytical, logic and pattern-driven historical side of the brain as well as the creative side, to find more and better options, ideas and solutions. You were born with both sides of the brain — it is about time you put them to work. The more they work, the better they work!

When was the last time you exercised your creativity just for fun? Perhaps you paint, do crosswords, write funny stories, poetry or letters to friends, do puzzles, doodle, or go to see kid's films for fun. Perhaps you read unusual books about interesting topics. If you don't exercise your creative mind, you lose it — so get creatively fit today and do some creative exercise. As long as you are creating in some way and the activity takes your mind away from 'what is' into 'what could be' then you are exercising your creative mind. You will be surprised how much it will invigorate you, make you feel good and probably even make you smile.

Take this as a case in point … I recently had a lawyer in his mid-forties attend a workshop with a group of his colleagues, and after a short introduction I asked the group to write an imaginary story about their partners. In the morning tea break, he came up to me with a huge smile on his face and proceeded to say what a wonderful experience that particular writing exercise was. He told me he had forgotten how much he enjoyed writing when he was a kid, and that he hadn't done anything like that for years. The smile on his face and the enthusiasm in his voice said it all! So don't wait any longer; grab some paper, your CD player, the newspaper, a book, your wacky younger cousin or whatever it is that helps you unlock your creativity, and start exercising your creative mind!

Fear

Unquestionably the other major barrier to creativity is fear. Fear takes many forms — the fear of failure, of ridicule, of embarrassment, the fear of what others will think, and even the fear of success. Some of the fears that seem to be mentioned most often in my workshops are:

- fear of failing
- fear of hierarchy
- fear of ridicule
- fear caused by upbringing
- fear of what people will think of you
- fear of time
- fear of success
- fear of the past
- fear of stepping outside the comfort zone
- fear of money
- fear of deadlines
- fear of clients.
- fear of, 'It's just the way we do it'
- fear of being laughed at.

Feel free to add in your own.

If you look at the above list, what percentage of those fears do you think you could address if you really wanted to? In most workshops when I ask this question, the answer is generally 90% to 95%, although I often have groups agreeing that they could do something about 100% of the things on the list if they really put their minds to it. It is a little subjective, but essentially I wanted you to see that we are our own worst enemy when it comes to stifling our ideas and creativity for reasons of fear. As Walt Kelly's Pogo, hero of a popular comic strip, put it many years ago: 'We have met the enemy, and he is us.' The good news is that we can do something about removing these barriers.

If you talk to people who have succeeded in business or succeeded in life in some way, you will find that there is a common theme — they have all faced adversity and numerous set backs in their lives, but despite this they have continued to pursue their goals, whether this be in sport, business, their personal lives, and so on. In order to be creative, one of the key things that we need to do is take away our fear of failure. Did you know that Winston Churchill was a failure at school? John Major — conservative prime minister of England — was a high school dropout. Isaac Newton failed numerous exams. Albert Einstein flunked his admission exams in science. Thomas Edison was notoriously slow in school, and Charles Dickens, Mark Twain and US presidents Washington, Lincoln and Truman never went to college. Modern society would probably see these people as failures early in their lives, however they grew up to be the leaders of many great lands and inventors of many of the things that we see around us. All of these famous people have one common trait, and that is they removed the fear. They didn't care that they didn't have the education. They were thinkers, and they were prepared to find out what was logical and challenge it. They were prepared to break through their educational and social barriers and try new things. They had no fear of failure because they had an undying passion and commitment to their cause. I recently read the autobiography of Virgin founder Richard Branson, entitled *Losing My Virginity*. Branson has created one of the world's great brands, and he is yet another example of someone who succeeded by constantly pushing the boundaries, trying new things, investing in his dreams, and most importantly having no fear of failure.

Think about this — could you swim the first time you hit the water? No. You probably swallowed water, dog paddled up and back, went under and came back up, and tried and tried again. You knew that you wanted to swim, and you just went about trying as many times as was needed and in many different ways to achieve your outcome. In fact, when you tried to swim the first time it probably scared you witless, but you persisted and risked drowning in order to achieve your goal. So in many areas (not just swimming — how about walking, running and talking), particularly when you were young, you have repeatedly experienced failure and fear and have succeeded in defeating both and moved on to reach for greater things. Truly you shouldn't worry about failure; you should worry about the opportunities you miss when you don't even try! Maybe we should take a leaf out of basketball legend Michael Jordan's book. Jordan did not fear taking the match-winning shot time and time again, as he believed there would always be another opportunity in another game. Jordan was also a guy who trusted his ability and backed himself constantly. To eliminate the fear of failure, ridicule or embarrassment, we must trust ourselves and back our own ideas.

In order to succeed, you have to be brave enough to try, and to question new things and not fear situations not working out the way you planned. You have to be creatively fit to challenge ideas and keep trying things and keep working, and to not be afraid that someone is going to think, 'Ah gee that's a bit silly,' or 'That's a stupid idea that will never work,' or, 'That's going to fail.' You must have inner-confidence and a belief in your own ability to come up with ideas and see those ideas through. If you have a great idea and it doesn't work, don't worry; try another idea. Remember you have plenty of them. What is the worst that can happen if you come up with an idea that someone doesn't like? You disregard that one and come up with another one.

There was a young lady in one of my workshops once who at the start of the first session firmly believed that she was not creative. Justine believed that there were others in the company she worked for who were better qualified than her to come up with new ideas and problem-solve. After working with me in the workshop, Justine had completely altered her thinking with regards to her own creative ability. By the end of the two days, she had turned her whole belief structure around 180 degrees; she began to believe in her ability to be creative, and she felt ready to put the new tips and tools to work.

Interestingly, I received an email from Justine a week after that workshop relaying the following story. On returning to work, Justine was invited to a boardroom creative session to discuss a client brief. With Justine's new commitment to ideas and creativity she was certainly not short of ideas, however when she put forward a particular idea one of the other participants openly criticised it, saying, 'That won't work, we don't have the money.' Justine simply replied, 'That's okay, it's just one idea. I have hundreds of them.' This from a lady who just a week or so earlier did not even believe that she was creative! Once you lose the fear of embarrassment, ridicule, other people's opinions and speaking up, you will be amazed at what great ideas you can generate.

Think about the fears that up till now have created barriers for you. Think about the false beliefs, barriers, excuses or reasons that are preventing you from pushing beyond your current limitations and finding new ground. What are they? Are they real or just excuses? If you really put your mind to it, how many of those fears and excuses could you remove or simply ignore?

Here are two very valuable quotes to think about:

'Do the thing you fear most and the death of fear is certain.'
Mark Twain

'Fear is not the reason for quitting, it's the excuse.'
Denis E Waitley

All you need to do to change your creative world is to change the way you see it, and the only barrier you face is your own perception about thinking and creativity.

GET OUT OF THE OFFICE!

Next I want to ask you to think about where you have most of your ideas. Is it in the car, the gym, walking the dog, relaxing with friends, drinking in the pub, while cooking, at the movies, in the bath tub or even on the toilet (you may laugh, but you would be surprised how many times this is mentioned!)? I'm sure that you can relate to at least a couple of the places on the list, and that you have your own special places where your ideas and thoughts tend to flow. It is interesting to note that the locations on this list are generally places where people tend to be most relaxed. And did you notice that the workplace does not feature among them? But isn't your workplace where you spend most of your time and where you are expected to have your great ideas? Yes. Does this make sense? No, of course not! Unfortunately, the very nature of the work environment makes it unconducive to generating ideas, so to be more creative I would suggest that you spend more time out of the office.

One suggestion is that when in Rome, do as the Romans do. It is believed that the Romans said, 'Solve it while you walk', and having just been to Rome, I can tell you Romans do a lot of walking. When looking for a new idea or looking to solve a problem, hop out of your seat, push your way from the boardroom table, release yourself from the computer — and walk. Simply by standing up you increase the oxygen to your brain by 10%, and this can only be good in terms of finding new and creative ways of solving problems and generating new ideas.

Your mind works better creatively when it is relaxed and open to the things around you that stimulate you. Whether you are surrounded by crowds of people, sitting quietly under a tree, in a coffee shop, or even walking through the streets, you need to make the time to get out of the office and have the time and space in which to just think. When you wish to generate ideas and you are experiencing a mental block, get out of the office! I would suggest that you go and sit in the park and look at the people walking by; see what they are doing and how they do it. Alternatively, why not go for a walk around your local office block or pop into retail stores and try using all the things around you as stimulants. When you go out on weekends, go out with the attitude that you are looking for new ideas and opportunities. Observe how things work, and keep your eyes and mind open to suggestions and solutions.

Look at your own list of places as to where you are most likely to come up with ideas, and think about where it is that you have come up with your best ideas in the past. If it is in your back garden, then perhaps once a week you should go to work a little bit later so that you can grab a cup of coffee and sit in the back yard and spend some time just thinking about a new idea. Perhaps you can solve a problem that's been niggling at you, find a new way to do something, or just have a good old think about life! For me that special creative space is my home office. It is my sanctuary and the place where I do my writing and my thinking. I go there most days, put on my music, burn some incense, close the door, and start to imagine whatever it is that needs some thought. No matter how busy my day might be or whether my mind is moving in many different directions, once I settle into my space I find it quite easy to focus and create.

When you are relaxed you think better. In the office, most people are generally trying to do two or three (or even four) things at once. Does this scenario sound familiar — answering the phone whilst checking your emails, flicking through your diary and pulling out that file before the next meeting ... whilst also trying to shovel a sandwich into your mouth! With all the tension, distractions and stress in the office, it is little wonder that the brain cells are not producing great ideas. This is one of the reasons that company retreats and strategic planning sessions, if done effectively, can be so rewarding. Retreats and planning sessions are generally undertaken in unfamiliar surroundings, they are relaxed, people have time to think proactively, and new and different triggers for ideas surround them. No wonder people find them stimulating and helpful for coming up with lots of great ideas and addressing potentially serious and often complex issues. If only we were given access to that type of situation more often!

I was watching an interesting documentary not long ago on the wonderful actor and activist Danny Glover. You would probably know Danny from many of his terrific roles in films such as *Lethal Weapon* 1 to 4, or possibly from his amazing contribution to numerous causes and charities in the USA. During the documentary, the presenter interviewed Mel Gibson, Danny's co-star on the *Lethal Weapon* films, and the series director Richard

Donner. Both of these men commented on Danny's sleeping habits and the fact that he could sleep anywhere. Mel Gibson even went as far as saying that Glover could sleep standing up between takes! They began calling Danny 'Horizontal Glover', as between scenes he used to just lean back in his seat and drop off to sleep, but when they were ready to shoot he would spring to life and get ready for action. Richard Donner said: 'Danny dozes off for three minutes, and when he wakes up he snaps to work and comes up with some really innovative ways of doing the scene.' Perhaps that is Danny's way of getting himself relaxed and letting his subconscious mind do the thinking for him. Either that, or he's just really tired!

Robert Frost once said, 'An idea is a feat of association.' When you take yourself away from the computer screen, boardroom or your workstation, you can usually help yourself to a lot more associations. Call them associations, stimulants or triggers, what we are really looking for here are items, events, people, colours, shapes or designs that will activate our creative minds. Not only will you be more relaxed away from your office or desk, which in itself is critical, but you will also be immersed in surroundings that can take you to places that you may not have drawn associations from previously. Are you stimulating your freethinking mind? Can you draw interesting associations in your current environment? Can you draw ideas from around your workspace? If not, then know that it is not hard to fix; you just need to get out of the house or office! Go for a walk, visit a bookstore, go sit in a coffee shop, or visit a shopping mall.

A good friend of mine is a singer songwriter who lives close to me in Sydney. His name is Drew McAlister. Drew has a publishing deal with a record company for his song writing, and I am always quizzing him about how he comes up with the concepts and ideas for his songs. Not surprisingly, it's not in a boardroom or an office that he gets his ideas, rather it is out on the street, in bars, shops or wherever life is taking place. Drew and I went away together for a bull riding rodeo weekend in Rockhampton in North Queensland a couple of years ago. The night before I arrived, Drew stayed at the old hotel in the main street — it's known as the Great Western and it is the favoured watering hole for all of the local cowboys. The next day, Drew and I were having a drink at the bar of the hotel and he told me about an old timer that he had met the night prior. This old guy had been through World War II, he had worked on the railroads all of his life, he had been married to his wife for 60 years, and he had several children and grandchildren of whom he was very proud. He had so many stories to tell, and Drew was all ears.

A few months later I caught up with Drew and he had written a great song called *Not the Man I Want to Be.* I asked him how he went about writing this one. He said he was sitting in his apartment and getting nowhere; he had a few ideas floating around but it wasn't coming together, so he decided to go to lunch. Sure enough, over lunch at the cafe it came to him, and it is a wonderful song written about the old guy in North Queensland. It made me think about how corporate types sit in their rather sterile office environments and hope to come up with a great idea for their product or service. They should be out in the streets and in the stores where their customers are shopping or their services are being provided. On a more personal level, think about the process you go through when buying a present for a friend. Have you ever had a great idea come to you when you were already out shopping for the present, and it wasn't necessarily even close to what you were originally looking for? By going out into the shopping environment you are filling your mind with triggers and alternatives for the present idea that, either alone or often combined with other suggestions and thoughts, enable you to come up with that great idea.

You may be thinking that my suggestions about getting out of the office may be all very good in theory, but your boss will just laugh at you if you suggest that you are heading off to the beach for a little thinking time. It is true that many senior managers cannot yet see the value in getting some of their employees out of the usual work environment, however it is still worth giving it some thought to see if you can come up with a solution that will work both for you and the company or individual you may work for. Here are a couple of suggestions …

Helen works for a company that permits employees to work from home if they have an important, high-priority job to do and they need some quiet time away from the office in order to complete it. Helen gradually began to stay a little longer at home in the back garden after completing her task, and she used that time to do her thinking. She watered the garden and proactively thought about an issue, and then when she returned to work she justified the time spent by producing the required work and then discussing the other ideas that she had come up with. In this way, she was able to gain a degree of confidence from management that the time she spent thinking (and often it was only an extra twenty or thirty minutes) was a worthwhile investment and that she was able to provide ideas and suggestions that could prove useful to the company.

Another alternative if you really cannot get any additional paid time for thinking is to use your lunch hour. This is your time, so why not just disappear for half an hour or so to think about any issues, challenges or opportunities that may have presented themselves recently. You can sit on a bench, wander the streets and people-watch, visit a bookstore or coffee shop, or simply lie on the grass in the park and visualise what it is that you need to think about.

I had the pleasure of having coffee one Saturday morning with Bill Miller, the brother of one of Australia's best known film directors, George Miller, who has been involved in such smash hits as *Babe*, the *Mad Max* series of films, *Dead Calm* and *Lorenzo's Oil*. During the course of our morning coffee, I asked Bill how George came up with the ideas for the very successful films they have conceived, directed and produced.

It turns out that the idea for the film *Lorenzo's Oil* came about one weekend when George was flicking through a newspaper at home and he came across a story about a man struggling to find a cure for the terrible disease that was afflicting his son. The story really moved George, and after doing further research and investigation into this real-life story, *Lorenzo's Oil* was conceived, and the movie ended up starring Susan Sarandon and Nick Nolte.

The basis for the story of the film *Babe* came about when George was listening to the in-flight entertainment on a plane from Sydney to London. One of the channels on the in-flight entertainment included an interview with a woman who was reviewing the children's book *The Sheep Pig* by Dick King-Smith. What captured George's attention was the enjoyment and laughter that was generated during that interview. On arriving in England, George was intrigued enough to search out a copy of the book in a local bookstore. He loved what he read, and he endeavoured to buy the rights to the story. This developed into what we all now know as Babe.

These two examples just reinforced my view that the people who make the best use of their creativity are those who are always on the lookout for opportunities. Generally speaking, these people don't do it consciously, it is actually done subconsciously. But the fact remains that they know ideas are all around them and they allow their subconscious to always be open to possibilities. Since we are on a movie tangent, I guess you could say it is a bit like what Kevin Costner is told in the film *Field of Dreams*; 'If you build it, they will come,' but in this case you could say, 'If you believe, the ideas will come.' The ideas will come, but you need to be open enough to new ideas around you in the first place, and you also need to have enough courage to do something with those ideas to turn them from ideas into reality. Many people have great ideas in the shower. It is the person who gets out of the shower, towels off and does something with it that is the true creative thinker. There are many more sensational and innovative films yet to be produced by George Miller and his production company, and you can be sure that the same process will be used in order to generate these original films. George Miller may be a highly respected and successful Hollywood director but he started off just like you or me.

Remember, wherever you may go and whoever and whatever you may want to be, get out of the office and be stimulated and open to new and innovative ideas!

BRING OUT THE CHILD WITHIN

I believe that children provide probably the best and most pure examples of the creative mind at work. When children are young they are totally unaware of what is possible, how they are supposed to do things or what the rules are, and they really couldn't care less what other people think of them or their actions.

Imagine if we could capture that special creative quality of children and harness it so that we carried it into our adult lives. Imagine being able to look at something as if it were the first time we had seen it rather than through eyes that perceive all of the barriers and preconceived hurdles and objections most people carry with them through life. Imagine being able to replicate the inquisitive nature of a child so that you would constantly want to question things, try things and meet new people. Do you know people who can participate in conversation after conversation and yet never ask a question, people who go through their lives never stepping out of the box and trying something new, never pushing themselves or questioning their beliefs? What happened to the child inside us that used to be like that and was not afraid of anything? It's time to bring that child back for a visit!

One of my favourite actors is Robin Williams, who I believe is one of the movie industry's greatest creative minds. In most workshops I run, I refer to a scene from one of his films called *Jack*, the story of a ten-year-old boy named Jack who is growing up in the body of a forty-year-old. As you can imagine, the situation itself would create some interesting dilemmas for any young boy in the schoolyard. There is a particular scene that I think is wonderful in this film. It is when Jack's best friend Louis is asked to read out his story about what he wants to be when he grows up. Although Louis is not exactly sure what he wants to be when he grows up, he says he does know who he wants to be like, and that is his best friend, the big guy, Jack. Louis says, 'He's only ten, but he looks much older. He's like the perfect grown-up 'cause on the inside he's just a kid. He's not afraid to learn or try things or to meet new people, the way most grown-ups are. It's like he's looking at everything for the very first time, because he is. Most grown-ups just want to go to work and make money, and show off to the neighbours.'

There are so many lessons from children that we should learn or remind ourselves of. Take for example the inquisitive nature of children and the propensity of children for asking questions — why don't adults ask more questions of themselves and others? Children don't have any preconceived notions about what they should and shouldn't do, so they will try new things. They are brave and adventurous, and they live life to its fullest. They charge through life at 100 miles an hour from sun up to sun down when they can go no more. They rest overnight and when that new day dawns, they are ready to do it all over again. Be prepared to have some fun with creativity and approach it like a child would — don't take it too seriously. When kids are creating they laugh, giggle and constantly fool around, all of which is great for the soul. Please remember it's okay to have a good laugh, to doodle on pads and to let your hair down a bit when creating. Laughter is a great creative stimulant … in fact it's a great stimulant for life, full stop!

It has been suggested that kindergarten and primary school teachers score very well in creativity tests when compared to other occupational groups. The world of the preschool child is filled with fantasy, fun, exploration and trial and error, and if you take the time to interact with these young, creative minds you can share in their world. If you have the opportunity to just sit and watch children, look for their inquisitive nature, their fearless approach and their thirst for the unknown, and think how that could apply to your own creative world. Think about what tips you can take from them to enhance and invigorate your own innovative mind.

One way to interact with children is through games and activities. A fun activity you might like to try is to look at the sky and ask a child what they think the clouds look like to them. Try to see what they are seeing;

imagine it as they see it, and then ask yourself what you see. Do it lying on your back on some grass, and just gaze to the heavens and let your imagination soar.

Have a look at the drawings of faces in the colour section in the middle of the book. These are the sorts of drawings that you would expect to see behind a proud parent's desk at work or on the fridge door at home with the name of their son or daughter written on the top or bottom corner. These works of art are generally proudly exhibited because the child has created them, and it is to be hoped they are also useful to remind us to pause from time to time to appreciate that there are things in their life more important than work.

The drawings are, however, a little different — they were in fact created by company CEOs, product managers, marketing executives and financial controllers during a workshop I undertook in Sydney a few years ago. The drawing exercise is really fun to do, and it constantly delights me to see people having a laugh when they are doing it. I gave these busy, responsible people the permission, the time and the opportunity to create and to bring out the child that is in all of us, and look at the results! Give yourself permission on a regular basis to bring out the child within — that child is still there in you somewhere, just waiting for the opportunity to be allowed out to play! The reason the pictures are so creative is that during the exercise I had them take away the barriers to creating. They are not typical faces that people would draw, given time and instructions. I put the music on really loud, and had them draw as fast as they could, so that they would simply draw whatever comes to mind, as a child would. They had no time to sit and think about what a normal, traditional, logical face would look like.

Like the child within us, the ability to be creative is still there in all of us; it has just been suppressed by our own self-doubt, our self-talk, the environment in which we work or live, or even our busy day-to-day lifestyles. I would encourage you to break out of your daily routines and beliefs and start to bring out the kid within you. Take your shoes off at lunch and take a walk in the park on the grass (my favourite scene from *Pretty Woman*), throw a ball around the office, paint, draw, laugh, have your boardroom meetings sitting on cushions on the floor. That's right, kick your shoes off and sit on the floor for your meetings. Better still, have your meeting at the zoo, the beach, or sitting in a park with cupcakes and red cordial.

Whenever I run workshops, I carry with me a certain number of toys for the people in the room to play with, such as play dough, plush toys, bubble makers, rubber balls, slinkies or Nerf toys. Although people may giggle and act as if it's not grown-up to play with the toys, most times they can't wait to get their hands on them and show them to their friends. Sound familiar? It's just the sort of thing we would do when we were kids. I love that, and encourage it at every opportunity.

I was once working with an association made up of thirty security companies. We were away in the mountains, and they had taken two days out of their working week to design their strategic plan for the next ten years. Now these people were all hard-nosed security industry representatives who had seen it all before, which is exactly the sort of challenge that I love. On the first day, the team walked into the room, which I had filled with toys and colour. For the first couple of hours they were very reserved, however by lunchtime on that first day they were completely comfortable with the surroundings, with me, and with the toys. In fact they loved the toys and they were never out of someone's hands. The workshop was a great success for the association, and interestingly a couple of the members of the association borrowed several toys to take to their next meeting! A few weeks later, one of the companies whose representatives had attended this workshop booked me for a planning session. This was the largest security company in the industry. It was a small gathering of just eight people, all of whom were managing directors of a division within this company. As they were the senior managing directors of this very large organisation, I felt they would be all business, so on this occasion I left the toys in the car. Well, the first guy entered the room and the first thing he asked was, 'Where are the toys?' You could have knocked me flat with surprise. I learnt a valuable lesson as I walked back to the car that day; you are never too old, too senior or too stuffy to think and play like a kid again.

One of my creative heroes is PT Barnum, the great American circus showman whose imagination, courage and creativity were boundless. Barnum was the man who coined the phrase 'The greatest show on earth' for his giant three-ring circus. In a movie about the life of PT Barnum (*Barnum*, 1986), Burt Lancaster, who plays Barnum, recounts the story of his grandfather who was the first to plant the seed of imagination into his young grandson, Phineas Barnum. In one particular scene, Phineas's grandfather gives his young grandson an island called Ivy Island. When the two of them go to visit the island, Phineas sees nothing more than a swamp-covered plot of dirt, littered with the debris of old carts, boats and rubbish and surrounded by water. Phineas feels cheated, but his grandad disagrees: 'As I stand here, you know what I see Phineas, I see a moated castle with knights in armour and maidens fair, I see savage Indians that only you and I can tame. I see magnificent and fearsome jungle beasts ... it's whatever you want it to be. *Imagination is the elixir of life and the seed of greatness.* I planted it in you. You must nurture it, protect it from the beast that will feed on its tender shoots; you must nourish it, give it room to grow and then when you are ready to harvest it, you will be the richest man in the land.'

It is to be thought — given his extraordinary and unique life — that young Phineas Barnum took that particular lesson from his grandfather to heart. *Imagination is indeed the elixir of life and the seed to greatness.* Nurture and nourish **your** seed and give it room to grow. Each and every time I watch the movie *Barnum* it inspires me to use my imagination and to find the next great idea, it excites me to want to do better, to ask more and better questions, and to find a new way to do things and not to be content with the way things are. It is important to have your own movies, books or friends that can inspire you once in a while and re-ignite your creative flame and initiate some new and exciting questions. Think about who or what your own personal stimulants are that you can call upon when you need that *creative espresso* ... that short, sharp jolt of creativity.

'Youth is a wonderful thing.
What a crime to waste it on children.'
George Bernard Shaw

PPC

I would like you to take a look at the following numbers and tell me what you notice about them ...

1 + 1 = 2

2 + 4 = 6

5 + 2 = 6

4 + 1 = 5

6 + 1 = 7

2 + 2 = 4

If you are like the majority of people in our workshops, the first thing about the numbers to receive comment is the fact that one of the additions has an incorrect answer (5 + 2 does not equal 6). Why is it that the majority of people choose to point out the incorrect answer first? There were many other things about the numbers that you could have commented on, such as the fact that they are all under ten, they are all additions, and so on.

The reason that the incorrect addition caught your eye is that our education and upbringing have taught us to think in a certain way. Society, our schooling system, our university system, education and business have all taught us to identify the things that aren't right. When most people look at an exam paper or when they proof-read a document for example, the first thing they generally do is go through and look for mistakes or critique it based on what is wrong with it rather than what is right about it. This can have a very detrimental effect on our creativity and the generation of ideas. In order to create a culture in which people are willing to give new ideas a chance to live, and in which individuals see the good in ideas before coming up with the reasons as to why perhaps the idea may not be suitable, I have developed a very simple approach to ideas called PPC, which stands for Positives, Potentials and Concerns.

The central concept of PPC revolves around the benefit gained by looking initially at all the positive things about an idea or concept; that is, what is great about the idea. Once this has been fully explored then you should consider what the potentials of the idea might be, before finally exploring the concerns. So if somebody comes to you with an idea or you are reviewing some work or looking for a new way to do something, the first thing that you would look at is all the positives; that is, all the things that are right about it and all the things that are good. Explore it as much as possible. Having done that, then step back and say what could be great with this — the potentials. For example, you might say, 'If we made the right steps here, and took the right moves there, this could be great about this idea.' Then finally you move on to critique it and consider all the things that might not be great, or anything that might be worrying to you.

Think about how this approach would change the way you think about ideas and how it would stimulate and foster a more creative environment. Say for example your assistant Mark comes to see you about an idea he has had over the weekend. He comes into the office all excited and looking forward to sharing his idea with you. He explains his idea to you and shares the whole concept. The first thing you may instinctively want to do is to go straight to what is wrong with the idea: 'Well Mark, it's not going to work because this is wrong with it and that is wrong with it, the boss would never go with it, the budget is not right, the timing is wrong … blah, blah, blah.' If you take this approach, think about how Mark is going to feel when he leaves your office. Is Mark going to walk away feeling good about himself and his idea, and is he going to feel comfortable coming to you again with more ideas on other topics or issues in the future? It depends on how confident he is, but probably not.

If, however, you apply the principles of PPC, the process with Mark would look something more like this: firstly you would have acknowledged all the things that were positive about Mark's idea. There were some very valid points; you liked these things about it, you liked that Mark had come to you with his suggestions and ideas — all the positives. You might then look at Mark's ideas and work through those things that don't quite work currently but that could have some potential down the track: if we changed the timing of this plan it could be great, if we altered this part it could be great, and so on and so on. Lastly, you would address the concerns, the issues that may be worrying you about the idea and the things that Mark may need to put some more thought into for next time. Do you think that Mark's experience in this case would be a far more positive one than with the first approach? Hopefully he will go away thinking, 'I have some more work to do on it and the idea may not work in this instance, but essentially I feel good about myself and I am going to keep coming back with new ideas,' rather than stopping because they aren't given an appropriate hearing.

PPC is a very simple but very powerful tool that you can use to foster a creative environment for you and those around you, and I have found that it is one of the favourite take-outs from my workshops. Because of the simplicity of the approach, it very quickly trains you in a new way of thinking, and it is a great process to allow you to respect newborn ideas and give them a chance to fly. Soon you will find yourself starting to say to yourself, 'What's positive about this idea?' and so on before you critique it, without having to formally go through the process each and every time.

In the previous chapter we discussed self-talk. PPC can even help train you to work through your own ideas, evaluate them in a less critical way and present them to yourself in a positive framework. I have worked with companies and individuals where PPC has had a lasting impact, and it is now routine for all positives and potentials of an idea to be explored before looking at any concerns. This has created a much more open, positive and creative environment because everyone knows that they and their ideas are going to get a hearing. Also you might want to try it at home when you are discussing ideas and thoughts with your partner and children — it works just as well at home with the family as in the workplace, and with the same positive results!

Give it a try; it is simple, yet PPC is a very powerful tool.

CHEATING IS GOOD

I found the following quote framed and hanging in an office corridor. It is an actual quote from the US Patent Office: 'Everything that is going to be invented in the world has been invented.' The caption underneath then went on to say, 'If this were true, we would still be sitting in the dark.'

Quick quiz for you — who said, 'Greed is good, greed works, greed is right'? (The answer is at the end of the section.) I have to agree with the sentiment, but I believe that it needs to be altered slightly to read, 'Cheating is good, cheating works, cheating is right!' In my training sessions, I always open with this line on my flipcharts because I want people to know that it is okay to borrow ideas from others to see if we can make them better. I don't mean to say that it is acceptable to steal ideas — that I do not agree with (although some would say there is a case for this if you are in direct competition with the other person or company). But if you are looking for a new 'look' for your home, don't you go through magazines to see what others have done and borrow their concepts? There are many shows on television currently showing us how to improve our finances, homes, gardens, cooking and holiday plans. We borrow ideas from these shows, and most would say this is a form of cheating because we are taking their ideas and making them suit us ... that is, making them better.

In many cases, a new product is an improvement on a similar concept in the same category or in fact a different category. We are fortunate at our training room, called 'The Vault' in Sydney, that we have a small retail/ entertainment precinct right at our front door. There are restaurants, coffee shops, a cinema, a music store, a bookstore and a few clothing retailers just around the corner. Quite often if a group of sales people, say from a security or computer company, are looking for new service or sales ideas for their industry, I will give them a couple of dollars each and ask them to go to the coffee shop, order a coffee, sit down and just watch the service. Although you may think that the coffee shop service has nothing to do with security or computers, workshop attendees often find that they can use the experience as a valuable springboard to an idea that is appropriate for their industry. I ask them to sit there like detectives, asking themselves what is great or not great about the experience and how they could apply the same principles to their industry. What are they doing that is great, or needs improving, and what can they learn from the service they received today?

Just recently I was running a session for one of Australia's most successful magazines, which specialises in decorating ideas for the home and garden, and the goal of the day was to generate story ideas for their publication for the upcoming year. We had spent the morning at The Vault doing many of the exercises in this book, so I sent them outside for a change of scene. They were put into groups of three and set an assignment — they had twenty minutes to find twenty story ideas from the shopping area next to The Vault. They were sent to a music store, a bookstore, fashion shops, a kid's playground and an ice cream store. Sure enough, each group came back with their twenty ideas in the twenty minutes allocated. A few even brought back sample ice creams! They were delighted to have so many ideas in such a short period of time, and the stimulation received from the other unrelated retailers was used really effectively to spark their imaginations.

The same tools can apply to the workplace — why not use the open market place as a springboard to improve your business and new production ideas? There is a great deal to be gained by walking around with your eyes open to all sorts of possibilities. I think movies, books, magazines and music offer many opportunities for the astute creative mind that is open to possibilities. When I set about creating a unique environment for corporate training and development, The Vault, there were two movies that provided the inspiration. The first was the film *Big* starring Tom Hanks, and the other was *Patch Adams* starring Robin Williams. Both films inspired me to build a better place for thinking, a place where people could come, drop their shoulders, relax, play a bit, have fun, and create. The Vault has been described in the press as a kindergarten for grown ups … exactly the concept I was after! I think Patch would be proud. In a way, you could say we cheated by taking the principles and theory from these two great movies and bringing them to life, but as you can see they are quite different concepts. There is a picture of The Vault in the colour section in the middle of the book.

The Vault is an old bank, and it sat vacant for six years. People would walk past and think 'vacant bank', but then one day I walked past and thought 'that would be a great workshop venue'. It's about being able to see and visualise possibilities that other people can't.

I have to say it is very amusing to see people's reactions in creative sessions when I tell them that it is okay to cheat. Quite often if a group is stuck for ideas in a session, I tell them to wander around the room, check out what the other groups that seem to be doing well are doing, then cheat by enhancing their ideas and making them into something better. Some people really do take to this concept like a duck to water, others however still find this concept very hard to accept and will defend their work by throwing their arms over their ideas so no-one can steal them. The choice is up to you — perhaps these people who find the concept of cheating difficult would prefer to think of it not as cheating but just as embellishing what's there, enhancing it, piggybacking it, or just using it as a stepping stone.

There is a great book called *Solutions Focus* written by UK-based Mark McKergow and Paul Z Jackson. I have done a number of sessions with Mark and I really enjoy his principles. In the book, Mark and Paul talk about the fact that when faced with a problem, often the solution lies within something that you are already doing well. Rather than dwell on the problem, they explore what has been going well and ask what else can be done in that light to make it better. It is a little like the cheating concept — take what is there already that may have merit and make it better. You may be looking at your own personal situation and looking at what a friend may be doing to get more time off, and cheat by applying the same principles to your own world, or it may be used more in a work sense where you take what another company is doing in a totally unrelated field to attract new customers, cheat, and do the same thing in your industry.

Some people think that for an idea to have any merit it has to be totally original. Many of the big ideas today sprang from another idea, or if you like, people cheated. So don't think that every idea you have has to be totally original. It is fine to take what is already there and simply make it better, and people and companies are doing it every day. Many original ideas are just an idea that someone else had, made better, so remember my motto … cheating is good, cheating works, cheating is right!

(Who said 'greed is good'? It was Michael Douglas playing Gordon Gecko in the movie *Wall Street*.)

KEEP A JOURNAL

There is a saying:

> *'Ideas are like a bird in a tree. They are great*
> *while you have your eye on them but the minute*
> *you turn away they are gone forever.'*

Ideas can indeed be very elusive if you don't get them down on paper right away! Have you ever had a great idea about something, and then your conscious mind turns to something else and you try to think back to what you were thinking of and suddenly it's gone forever. It can be very valuable to keep a good quality, hardcover journal to store all of your ideas, dreams, goals and in fact anything at all that you think you might want to keep for future use.

Jim Rohn, American's foremost business philosopher, has said, 'Don't use your mind for a filing cabinet. Use your mind to work out problems, and find answers; file away good ideas in your journal.' Your head has enough to store as it is; just buy yourself a good hardcover journal and make it your filing cabinet. Take this journal with you to seminars, workshops or anywhere that you are going that may generate some good ideas, quotes or points of interest. That way, when you think back to those seminars or guest speakers you saw, you know exactly where any ideas or thoughts would have been written down from those workshops. The other advantage is that after a year or two, you can go through your journal and harvest dozens of great ideas, quotes and one-liners that you can then use throughout your own day, and they have been just sitting there waiting for you to pick them up. After a while you will have amassed such great information in your journals that they can become your ultimate self-help, how to, what if books!

For nearly ten years now I have kept a leatherbound hardcover journal for ideas. I have taken it to every conference and seminar I have been to in that time (thankfully it is a large book!). It is now a treasure trove of ideas, quotes, sayings, exercises and content for me to use in workshops and conferences. If I have seen someone speak in that time my notes and doodles are in that journal — I record interesting names, ideas, goals, dreams, concepts for workshops and even contacts of people I meet in the sessions. So don't let your ideas, thoughts or interesting quotes end up in the back pocket of your jeans in the wash — write them in a journal and keep them on hand for when you may need them.

There is another reason why I keep my journal full of book summaries — I know I have my summaries all in one place and the repetition of doing them helps my learning. It may seem like a fairly straightforward task and not all that necessary for a couple of books, but once you have read twenty, thirty or forty books and you have your notes for all these books stored in one location, your journal becomes a valuable resource. I am constantly amazed at how much great stuff I have stored up in my journal, and when I need to present a workshop or a keynote I can simply go to my journal, flick through it and easily pull out great, pertinent quotes, references, points or sayings and drop them into my presentation. It saves me having to go back through lots of books looking for the best quotes, as they are all in my journal ready to go.

WHAT DOES FOOD HAVE TO DO WITH CREATIVITY?

I've been studying the eating habits of people in workshops for over five years, and anyone who has attended one of my sessions knows the importance I place on food. I am not a nutritionist, a doctor, a naturopath or a dietician; I am a creative facilitator who has observed the difference food makes in the conference, coaching, seminar and workshop environments. This information I uncovered from real-life experience and experimentation, but it is backed up by some sound scientific study. I have been watching people's reactions towards food for many years in my workshops and I am convinced that what we are about to discuss will make a massive difference to your sessions or meetings.

Traditionally workshop venues and conferences serve mints, lollies, pasta, pastries and sandwiches as part of their session menu. I'm dead against this, as the massive amounts of sugar that is provided by these carbohydrates and sweets means not only that people experience peaks and troughs in their energy levels, but it also leads to sleepy, tired and unproductive attendees.

There was a story recently in a leading Australian newspaper, *The Australian*, that stated one in three executives sleeps during meetings.[4] In my view, this situation arises either because the presenters are boring or because the attendees are having far too much sugar in their diet during the sessions. Without the massive sugar overloads that traditionally occur at many conference facilities, it has to be said that even the dullest of presenters will hold the majority of the audience, but if you combine ineffective presenters with loads of sugar you might as well pull out the doonas. The best creativity

---

4   *The Australian* newspaper, October 2000.

comes when you have clarity, and massive amounts of carbohydrates will not lead to any great clarity; in fact, I can set my watch by how long it takes for people to start getting heavy eyes and losing concentration after a serving of large sugary tarts or thick croissants for morning tea. After twenty minutes, the yawns start, and of course the group's productivity begins to fall away and you lose whatever contribution they might have made during that session.

So what is the solution? How do you feed people to keep them awake and energised during your creative sessions and presentations? Your body is a high-performance machine and it needs high-performance food. Don't serve mints, don't provide lollies, don't have sandwiches for lunch and don't serve big, thick, sweet cakes and pastries for morning and afternoon tea. Instead, serve high-energy food — for morning tea perhaps serve light cookies, and for lunch freshly grilled chicken pieces with salad or a nice piece of fish and vegetables. Finally, ensure there is fresh fruit available for people to munch on through the day, such as whole apples, bananas and pears. It is possible to serve this great, healthy energy food without fuss for the same price as the lavish plates of sandwiches that people have come to expect, and what's more, it is tastier for the participants. It sounds funny, but the food you serve has an enormous impact on the outcome of your sessions. So think about it, plan for it, and reap the rewards.

I have provided a sample of what I have been talking about with regards to a healthy workshop menu:

Sample menu

On arrival
Fruit, water, juice, tea (herbals as well), coffee

Morning tea
Light cookies (low sugar), fruit, water, juice, tea, coffee

Lunch
Chicken or fish with salads or vegies (no bread or rolls, no pasta, no steaks!)

Afternoon tea
Light cookies or fruit cake (low sugar), fruit, water, juice, tea, coffee

No mints or lollies in the room; instead serve fruit all day in whole pieces. (People don't need those mints, they only eat them because they are there!)

I am a stickler for a healthy workshop menu such as the one above, and I only serve this type of food when we run workshops at The Vault and it is amazing how many people make a comment about the food. They notice the food because by around 3 pm or 4 pm they are still feeling great and have the energy to continue to contribute to the discussion. Conference organisers seem to think that because they are going to a conference they should serve naughty foods, like cakes, lollies and chocolates. But if one in three people sleep through meetings and workshops, you are *wasting* one-third of the money you have just spent on the conference because you fed them the wrong foods. People want to feel good at the end of a hard day. They want the energy to go home and do something with their own precious time. So put the right food into their engines.

Scientifically there is also considerable evidence to suggest a medical benefit that the right sorts of food can have on creative thinking. Lean proteins such as fish and chicken stimulate the transmission of neurotransmitters such as dopamine and norepinephrine to the brain, which in turn supports mental activity. These are known as the alert chemicals. To think more quickly, react more rapidly to stimuli, and feel more mentally energetic, cut down dramatically on carbohydrates and boost your protein intake. Protein contains tyrosine, the principle ingredient in dopamine and norepinephrine. The best sources of these proteins are fish, chicken, shellfish, legumes and soy-based products. If you combine your protein with salads and vegies for a healthy, brain-boosting meal you will also feel an instant kick in your energy levels. We should also consider increasing our intake of fish to two to three helpings per week. Fish is very important for the brain; it contains high protein levels, and also valuable oils and good fats, yet most of the population don't eat enough of it.

Now eating is a very personal thing and should be treated as such. I am not attempting to tell you how you should eat as there are loads of great books that can take you through the virtues of a well-balanced diet. All I am endeavouring to do is to show you how to maximise your thinking capabilities through a modified diet and how to improve the outcome of your conferences by serving the right menu. You can even apply the same principles on a daily basis to increase your productivity at work or at home if you so desire.

SLOW DOWN

Before each creative workshop I make it a practice to sit down with the client and discuss the expected outcomes and agenda for the session, as each session I run is designed specifically for that client and tailored to their needs and outcomes. One of the most common questions I hear from corporate clients is how long is the workshop. Generally speaking, they can run from a half to two full days, but naturally I can cover a lot more material if we have more time in which to work. It is surprising how many of these clients will ask me to condense two days' worth of work into one. They think that suddenly I can talk faster or that I should cram more information in so that they can wring more value from the workshop. The other suggestion I get is that perhaps we should forget about the section of the workshop dealing with belief barriers and an understanding of creativity, with a preference for just moving straight into explaining different tools to increase creativity. I find it amazing that corporations will pay a great deal of money to send their employees to a creativity workshop to stimulate creative thinking in their business, yet in that very session they want you to cram as much as you can in and throw lots of information at the people in the room, and expect them firstly to learn it all and secondly to take the time to think and ponder about how they might create better ideas in their life. They are kidding themselves!

These days the corporate world is full of deadlines, to-do lists, multi-tasking and time-poor executives. In order to cope, employees are constantly being encouraged to improve their time management and attend priority management courses to enable them to cram more into their day. The sad thing is that each executive has exactly 168 hours in a week and no more, and there comes a point when they can't cram any more in. It is this cramming and 'get to the tools' ideology that is making it difficult for executives and the corporate world to come up with new ideas. Those who work in the corporate world need to slow down and take the time to sit under a tree or go for a walk around the block and ponder. If people learn to slow down and begin spending more time in the moment, they will begin to notice that they get more done, they are more organised, they will have better preparation, better ideas, and what's more they might actually enjoy the process. They will start to excel in their achievements and goals, and enjoy and appreciate each step of the journey.

One of the most widely read executive books is *The 7 Habits of Highly Effective People* by Stephen R Covey. In this book there is a section based on organising your day and working in one of four 'quadrants'. Stephen's solution to getting ahead of the time game is to spend more time in quadrant two where you do the things that are important but not urgent, such as planning, preparation and prevention. The same principles apply to creativity. We need to stop trying to cram more into our day, which is sucking the creativity out of us, and give ourselves more time to create, think and ponder. What is one good idea worth for your business? Depending on the size of your business, anywhere from hundreds to millions of dollars!

ENJOY A CREATIVE SORBET

In the book by sports psychologist Jim Loehr called *The Power of Full Engagement*, Jim talks about the rituals that the great tennis players undertake between points. He indicates that the research he has been shown demonstrates that the difference between the good players and the great players on the tennis circuit can be boiled down to the routines that the great players have between every point. He said the great players could drop their heart rate significantly between points because of the rituals they perform between points, and this gave them greater endurance as the match wore on.

A great example of this, he said, could be seen by looking at the on-court ritual of one of the world's great tennis players, Ivan Lendl. Between each point, Lendl would wipe the sweat from his brow on his arm band, knock the head of the racket on each of his heels, take sawdust from his pocket, bounce the ball four times, and visualise where he intended to hit the ball next. And he did this between *every* point. Doing so allowed him to rest, refocus and drop his heart rate, and this in turn gave him greater endurance than some of the lesser players who did not have a ritual such as this. Perhaps we should take a leaf out of Lendl's book and ask ourselves whether we should have a similar ritual in our lives. When do we take time out from our game ... the game of life? When do we rest, recuperate, and get set for the next point? Most of us just go on playing 24/7, year after year, without any rest between points, let alone games, sets or matches.

I was visiting with a friend of mine named Russell, the creative director of a very prominent and successful advertising agency in Sydney. During a briefing for the upcoming session I was going to run, he came out with the following statement, which reminded me once again of the Lendl story I had read in Jim Loehr's book: 'What our creative department needs is a creative sorbet.' I asked him for an explanation as to what he meant by that, and he said that his creative team works on so many projects during any given day that they are constantly going from one job to the next without a break. Not only are they having to change their thinking to accommodate the specific brief for each job, they also have a mind full of old ideas, stale thoughts and overall fatigue. Russell was searching for a way to cleanse the minds of his team between jobs, much like the way top restaurants serve sorbet between courses to cleanse the palette of the patrons. He thought it would be great to develop a creative sorbet to cleanse their minds before starting the next job for the day. What a great metaphor ... no wonder he is such a great creative director.

So what could a creative sorbet consist of? It can be anything from walking around the block, doing a crossword, lying on the floor of the office with your eyes closed listening to some relaxation music, to writing a fun, imaginative, fictitious story about a friend. Perhaps you could call a friend to throw some ideas around, read a few pages of a great novel, try a fun brainteaser, or spend ten minutes meditating. How you use your sorbet time is up to you, and it should be whatever works for you. The main aim is to cleanse your mind at regular intervals throughout the day, rather than just powering through the eight or ten — or even twelve — hours of your day without pausing for some 'me' time. If you pause between points you will find once again the part of you that wants to be the best it can be.

Make a note to also pause occasionally on weekends and to book yourself some proper down time by taking a holiday. If you work hard you deserve regular breaks — don't be a martyr by not taking holidays as it is not making the best use of your creative talents. Make the time to rest, regroup, dream and ponder, and there is no better time to exercise your creative spirit than on the weekend, or better yet, when on holidays!

Cleanse your brain and imagination and grab a creative sorbet each day!

GET SOME EXERCISE

To be healthy and promote wellbeing we all know that we should exercise daily and that we should eat the right foods and of course get adequate rest, and I believe these elements are also critical to enhancing creativity. I am not about to lecture you on your diet and physical exercise habits, but you should know that you will enhance your ability to generate ideas if you are eating well, getting some exercise and also plenty of rest. Just think about how much harder it is to come up with ideas when you have returned from a large, unhealthy lunch and you are feeling tired and lethargic, as opposed to when you have eaten well and you are well rested and alert. If you want to enhance your ability to turn out good ideas, get some rest, and watch what you eat.

Now quite apart from your body's general health and exercise, I want you to start thinking about exercising your brain. Consider how much money we spend on the outside of our heads — guys buy shaving creams, moisturisers, aftershaves, hair gels, shampoos and haircuts, and I am not going to even try to start with the ladies. My point is that we spend so much time and money on the outside of our heads, we should invest more time and money on the inside of our heads, and by that I mean good books, educational workshops, audio programs, information videos, newsletters, brain foods and other stimulants that encourage us to think. Most people are so busy on a daily basis that they do not take the time to sit down quietly and exercise the inside of their minds. You can exercise your mind simply through books, magazines, audio programs and the like, or by doing brainteasers, crosswords, puzzles or, simplest of all, holding a basic conversation with a friend or partner where you ask a few questions and really listen and think about the answers. We really do not spend enough time thinking, let alone exercising our creative minds.

In workshops when I pose a brainteaser such as, 'Explorers found two naked bodies frozen in the ice, one male and one female. When they looked at them they knew straight away that they were Adam and Eve ... How did they know?', people tend to roll their eyes and say, 'Oh I hate these things, I can never get them.' Little wonder, as with that kind of talk they are programming themselves for failure. The people who love them, and funnily enough seem to get them right, are the ones who say, 'Bring it on, I love these things, I always get them right', and are those who do them often and become good at them. It is like anything in life, whether it is golf, reading, painting, interior design or cutting hair; the more you practise it, the better you become. The same applies to thinking and creating — the more you practise and exercise the brain, the more efficient you will become with brainteasers like the one above. You need to be persistent and exercise your creative mind regularly. You will notice the difference in all sorts of areas in your life.

On New Year's Eve 2001, I was on the Gold Coast with some great friends. In the wee hours of the morning we were walking through an outdoor mall when we stopped to get a cup of coffee at a cosy coffee shop. The place happened to have a chequer board, which I thought was great, so I found a willing opponent and off we went. Now I hadn't played chequers for quite some time, and I wasn't setting out necessarily to win (although I am rather competitive), what I was really enjoying however was the feel of my brain ticking over as I tried to outmanoeuvre my opponent. Thinking about my next move as well as two or three moves ahead, whilst also considering my opponent's moves, was a different type of thinking to that in my normal day-to-day routine. It was a lot of fun and it was exercising my mind, which I really enjoyed. Why not try it now and then — you can read a book, or grab a newspaper and do the crossword, find a list of brainteasers, or play a game of chess, Scrabble or Pictionary. Maybe you can watch a quiz show and try to compete with the contestants, or turn on National Geographic channel and watch a story on a topic you would not normally gravitate to, and spend some time thinking about the topic or the story. Even better still, why not go and hang out with a bunch of inquisitive children who want to know 'why this' and 'why that'. Don't give up when you find it a little hard at first — persist and exercise that brain of yours.

Do you think that the sports heroes you admire got to where they are without practice? What about your favourite painter — did they get that good without practice? Creativity isn't any different. We must make ourselves creatively fit by exercising our minds over and over. When you go to the gym, the first few days are always hard, but if you persist and you do the hard yards, sooner rather than later you start to see results and suddenly the process is much more enjoyable. The more you exercise your mind, the more you will enjoy the challenge of creative thinking and the better you will become at it. Think to yourself each day, have I exercised ... my brain? This is exercise that you can really enjoy and do easily, so please have fun with it and don't take it all too seriously — just make sure that you are setting your mind to tasks and *thinking*! Do fun things like puzzles and game shows, perhaps even pick up a book on a topic you know nothing about and expand your knowledge base on that topic. I personally have set myself a target of reading a book a week each week for the last six years, and my best result is forty-eight books in a year. Normally I read non-fiction — business, finance, health and fitness, and biographies; however, I have decided to read a fiction book every fourth book just to exercise and stimulate my brain with something different.

Reading may not be your thing, but there will be something out there that will suit you and that will exercise that brain of yours. One young guy in one of my workshops is particularly innovative and he goes to his local pub every Wednesday night for a trivia night. He and a few of his mates gather at their local watering hole and play for prizes in a trivia competition. He says that even if they do not know the answer to a question, he and his mates think through the question, ponder the options and then have a go at the answer, rather than throwing their hands in the air and simply giving up as some of the other teams do. By going to these trivia nights he is having a great time, enjoying a few beers and exercising his brainpower, which is a great thing to do to stimulate your creativity!

So get out there and start being creatively fit!

(Back to the brainteaser — how did they know that the bodies were those of Adam and Eve? The two bodies did not have belly buttons!)

MUSIC

Music is a very powerful creative tool and has an important role to play in the stimulation of your creative mind and in generating ideas. Dr Georgi Lozanov in his pioneering work on the mind illustrated the brain-boosting power of music to great effect. Dr Lozanov found that rhythmic and soothing baroque music has a huge impact not only on our creative mind but also on our ability to absorb and recall information. Between the years 1600 and 1800, baroque composers such as Handel, Vivaldi, Bach and, perhaps the most celebrated baroque composer, Mozart, specifically set out to create music to lift the spirit and free the mind from day-to-day concerns. Baroque music's steady, stately tempo of approximately sixty beats a minute parallels the brain's wavelength when it is in the state of relaxed alertness, or what they call the alpha brain wave pattern. This state of relaxed alertness, claims Lozanov, forms a receptive state of learning and creating.[5]

Don Campbell, the co-author of a book called *Rhythms of Learning*[6], also claims that baroque music slows us down and encourages us to listen better because we are receiving at the body's preferred speed. He suggests that underneath music is a code of rhythm and sound that your left brain relates to, while the right brain relates to the texture of the sounds, and so the music

---

5   *Accelerated Learning for the 21st Century: The Six-Step Plan to Unlock Your Master-Mind* by Colin Rose, Dell, 1998, p183.

6   *Rhythms of Learning: Creative Tools for Academic Development* by Chris Brewer and Don Campbell, Zephyr Press, Tucson, AZ, 1991.

becomes a harmonisation of body, mind, heart and spirit.

Try it yourself and see what effect it has on your creative ability. The next time you would like to think about something or are looking for some new ideas, put on some baroque music — Bach, Vivaldi, Handel, Mozart or something similar. Or if you prefer, perhaps try something more recent that is recorded at about fifty or sixty beats per minute, such as Enya or Enigma. Most relaxation music available in stores is recorded at fifty to sixty beats per minute. Check out new age stores, health spas and the new world section of your music store. They will have music appropriate for what you are looking for. I use Native American flute music mostly, sourced from reservations in Arizona, Utah and the Dakotas in the USA (I have included a list of the artists that I like to play at the back of the book[7]), but it is also available through good record stores and via the web. The music will slow down your heart rate to about fifty or sixty beats per minute, the speed at which your heart rate parallels your brain waves in alpha state. In this very relaxed state, the mind is free to create and dream and is receptive to new ideas.

I will conclude this section with a poem from Henry Wordsworth Longfellow:

And the night shall be filled with music.

And the cares that infest the day

---

7   Appendix B: Blue Moon workshop CD recommendations.

Shall fold their tents like the Arabs

And as silently steal away.

I encourage you to use relaxation music to slow down from the day and give yourself the chance to relax and create.

THE STORY OF THE STATUE OF DAVID

To conclude this chapter I wish to share with you a story about the magnificent statue of David …

Perhaps you have been fortunate enough to have visited Florence in Italy to see the magnificent statue of David, sculpted by the famous renaissance artist Michelangelo. When he was first commissioned to create the statue back in 1501 as a symbol of courage for the city of Florence in a period of civic unrest, Michelangelo looked for many months for exactly the right piece of marble from which to carve his work. Finally he was entrusted with an old and partially worked block that had been quarried and begun some forty years earlier by renaissance sculptor Agostino di Duccio. It was a vast block of Tuscan marble eighteen feet tall, commonly referred to as 'the giant', which had stood abandoned for decades in the workshop of the Florentine cathedral and which was generally believed to be ruined marble.

For three years Michelangelo carved away at that block of marble, piece by piece, until those around him could begin to discern the outline of a human torso. Further work with sand, chisel and massage was required, until finally he pronounced that he was happy with the completed work — three years of hard work were finally over.

The evening finally came when the people were gathered in the public plaza of Florence, the Piazza della Signoria, for the unveiling of the statue. During the ceremony the white sheet that covered the statue was torn away, and the crowd was amazed at the beauty and magnificence of the David. A man approached Michelangelo and said, 'That is wonderful, how did you ever create something so special?' Michelangelo replied, 'It was actually quite easy. The David was always there, all I had to do was get rid of everything that was *not* the David.'

And so it is with creativity. Creativity and freethinking ability is there within all of us; in this book I am simply endeavouring to get rid of everything that is *not* the creativity! Hopefully the first half of this book will have begun the process of removing the disbelief, fear and uncertainty we all harbour with regards to our ideas and creativity, and also that little voice in our minds that tells us we are not creative. I have suggested some habits and processes that will assist you with building a more creative environment, and now I will move on and give you some practical tools or 'keys' to help you generate better ideas and more of them.

3 THE KEYS — TOOLS TO UNLOCK YOUR CREATIVITY

Now that we have discussed the key barriers to creativity and how to remove them and I have given you some suggestions as to how to foster a more creative environment, it is time to give you some practical, easy-to-use tools to make better use of that creativity inside you. Grouped together in this chapter, the tools I discuss should provide you with a 'key ring' full of suggestions as to how to maximise your creativity and generate better ideas and more of them. Enjoy!

THE KEYS

Let's start those ideas flowing with the power of your subconscious ...

Key 1: Using your subconscious

It's late on a Friday afternoon; you are working away at your desk and in walks the boss, who informs you that he wants you to come up with some great ideas for a client by Monday morning. What do you do?

The first tip I am going to give you is to 'forget about it'. That's right. Have you seen the movie *Donny Brasco*, in which Johnny Depp plays an undercover cop learning to be a New York gangster wise guy? His character is lying on the couch talking to two other cops, and he says that in wise guy talk there are six or seven different ways to say 'forget about it', and each way means something different. 'Hey ... forget about it.' Well in terms of creativity, when I say forget about it, it means exactly that. If you are looking for an idea or a solution to something, quite often one of the best and most powerful tools you can use is your subconscious.

Have you ever been sitting at a dinner party where there has been a table of eight or ten people, and over entree you are all talking about a movie and you can't for the life of you remember the name of the actress who played a particular role. By the time the dessert comes around the conversation has moved onto a completely different topic, but suddenly out of the blue you say, 'Demi Moore!' You have finally remembered the name of the actress from the discussion at entree!

Why does that happen? Well, you placed a question into your subconscious mind, and while your conscious mind moved onto a completely different topic of conversation, your subconscious mind went to work going through the files at the back of your mind to try and find the answer for you. The answer was there somewhere; you just couldn't recall it when you wanted to. You can use your subconscious in a similar way when you need to generate an idea for something. If ideas don't come to your mind straight away, then plant the problem into your subconscious mind, give yourself all the information you require to think it through, and then forget about it. Move onto something completely different, and you will find that your subconscious mind will start coming up with ideas for you when you least expect it. This tool can be particularly handy if you are preparing a presentation or if you are generating ideas for something and you can give yourself some time. Start to prepare for your presentation perhaps three, four or even seven days prior to the event, and place the outline into your subconscious mind. You will find that as each day passes you will start thinking of things to include in your presentation. I'm not sure I can tell you scientifically why this occurs, but I guess we don't actually need to know exactly how it works, we just need to believe that it does work. Trust your subconscious mind and forget about it.

If you are sitting at work looking for an idea or a way to do something differently and it is not happening for you then put down your pen, close the door to your office and go for a walk and forget about it, whether it is through town, through the suburbs or a walk at the beach. Come back an hour later and start thinking about it again. It is surprising how many times you will find your subconscious mind will find ideas and generate ideas and solutions for you while your conscious mind is busy thinking about something else. In fact, the creative subconscious mind works most effectively when the conscious mind is distracted and working on something else, leaving the subconscious to work through the issue without interference.

Quite often people are using their subconscious on a daily basis and they do not even know they are doing it. Take Elizabeth, a publicist friend of mine, for example. We were sitting having a chat one day when Elizabeth said that although quite often she has no thought as to what angle she will take with a particular story in the early part of the week, she knows that an idea will come to her by her deadline on the Friday. Naturally when Elizabeth said this it caught my attention, and I immediately asked how she could be so sure. Elizabeth said she just knows, and after years of doing it she has a firm belief that her subconscious will do the work and the ideas will … just come. The funny thing is that Elizabeth doesn't know exactly how it works, and she does not want to know — the important thing is that she knows and believes that ideas will come, providing you trust it.

It is also your subconscious at work when you get great ideas in your sleep. Whilst you are relaxed and resting, your creative subconscious is faithfully pouring over hundreds of thousands of files in your mind looking for the suitable solution to challenges. Then in the middle of the night when your subconscious believes it has the answer, it will wake you up with it. That is why many people choose to sleep with a small dictaphone or writing pad by their beds, so they can capture these precious ideas in the middle of the night. If this is something that happens to you on a regular basis, you may want to consider placing a dictaphone or a pen and pad near your bed for this very reason.

The good news is that your subconscious can also work for you when you are studying or learning new information. Here's an example of how you can program your subconscious to learn new information for you while you are sleeping:

1. Revise the new information prior to turning in.

2. Review the material briefly just before sleep.

3. Sleep.

4. Briefly review the information on waking up in the morning.

This subconscious learning routine was tested on two groups of students by researchers Jenkins and Dallenbach. Both groups of students spent the same amount of time learning a specific list of words. One group was tested after eight hours of daytime activity. They scored a 9% recall. The second group was tested after eight hours of sleep. They recorded a 56% recall![8] So as the saying goes ... sleep on it. If you are facing a challenge, why not let it sit in your subconscious while you are sleeping and then face it with new vigour next morning?

I can honestly say that I am not exactly sure how the subconscious mind works; I just know that it does, and that's the important part. Trust it. It is more powerful

---

8   *Accelerated Learning for the 21st Century: The Six-Step Plan to Unlock Your Master-Mind* by Colin Rose, Dell, 1998, p141.

than we can even try to imagine. The brain is said to have a capacity equivalent to the world's total telephone system in just one gram that's the size of a Smarty. We are believed to use just 1% of our brain capacity, so put it to work and … forget about it!

Key 2: Visualisation

Have you ever taken note of a professional tennis player before they are about to serve? They look down, bounce the ball a few times and get themselves set for the point. Or perhaps during the Olympics you might have noticed swimmers, gymnasts or even some of the track stars in an almost trance-like state as they prepare to compete. Chances are that these athletes were visualising the job ahead; they were drawing mental pictures in their minds as to what they were about to do and they were *seeing* themselves doing it well. Perhaps you could call it a dress rehearsal for the real thing, visualising a successful outcome prior to taking action.

It seems there are more and more stories of athletes who use the power of visualisation to achieve their goals. Jim Loehr, the sports psychologist I mentioned earlier in the book, has worked with tennis greats like Gabriella Sabitini and Jim Courier, and he teaches players to spend twenty-five seconds between points visualising a previously great shot, forgetting a bad one, relaxing, and then building for the next shot. Michael Jordan is another great advocate of visualisation. He replays the perfect shot over and over in his mind, and time and time again he sees himself taking that match-winning shot.

So when it comes time to take that pressure shot in a close game, it seemed so easy for him as he had taken that shot hundreds of times in his mind. The great ice hockey legend Wayne Gretzky always said that he would visualise where he believed the puck was going, not where it was currently, and Jack Nicklaus, one of the greats of the golfing world, uses a similar technique. With 100 professional golf championships to his credit, including 20 majors, he plays a mental movie before each shot — before he makes a putt, he sinks it in his mind first.

On a more personal level, I recall an occasion when the power and effectiveness of visualisation was demonstrated to me. I was flown to the Barrier Reef in North Queensland as the keynote presenter for a company that specialised in sales promotions. It was their annual get-together where they reviewed the year that had passed and planned ahead for the year to come. It was a fairly relaxed group of people in the most beautiful surroundings at a resort called Laguna Quays. There were around forty people in total at the conference and they were all working hard (and as you can imagine, playing just as hard!). On this particular day, I was invited to do a two-hour presentation to the group about freethinking and creativity. The managing director wanted the group to learn to push the limits to a greater extent and to find unusual angles on promotions that would excite their clients. He also wanted to encourage them to challenge each other, to take a step away from the norm and take some risks. The session was going very well, and I was discussing the power of visualisation and giving examples. There was positive feedback from the room about other occasions when individuals from within the group had used visualisation in the past to great effect. At this stage I had been presenting for just on an hour when I decided to try something a little different with the group to demonstrate the power of visualisation.

I had everyone in the room take off their shoes and lie on the floor. I turned the lights down and played some soothing music by Enya on the stereo system. I then proceeded to take the group on a guided medita tion (which I have included at the back of the book for you to use in your own sessions if you are interested)[9]. Once I had slowed their breathing and had them fully relaxed, I started to tell them a story in a slow, peaceful and soothing voice. As I led the group through the story, each of the participants in the room followed my journey in their own minds, each seeing it differently, the way they would visualise it. On completing the guided visu-alisation that only took ten minutes in total, I had them describe to each other what they had seen … with their eyes closed! It was amazing to hear the vivid descriptions that people shared with each other about what they had seen. It is a wonderful exercise to do with people to show the power and clarity of using visualisation as a way to see things and imagine things in our own minds, with our eyes closed.

Visualisation is not only a great tool to assist you in achieving your goals, it is also a wonderful tool to enable you to generate ideas. Creativity is all about find-ing stimulants and triggers that foster new ideas, and

---

9   Appendix C: Guided visualisation.

creative visualisation can be the catalyst to do just that. Creative visualisation is the process by which you create a picture of an opportunity, event or place in your mind, and this allows you to use the image to find stimulants from which to draw new ideas. Because humans are very visual creatures we tend to think in pictures, and so it makes sense that we can also create using pictures. Here's how it works …

Creative visualisation works best when you are relaxed and your mind is calm, so allow yourself to get comfortable, perhaps even move away from your normal work environment. You might like to sit upright, while some people will prefer to lie down or lean back in an armchair. When you are relaxed, close your eyes and just start creating a picture in your mind of what it is you wish to develop ideas for. Say for example you wish to come up with ideas for a birthday present for a friend. The first thing to do is to create a picture of that person in your mind and think about their daily routine. What do they wear to work? Where do they go? Picture what their desk looks like, who they meet, what their car looks like, when they go to a meeting, and so on. Or maybe think about them at home: picture what their bedroom looks like, what you can see them doing in their spare time, where they go, what they enjoy doing. Picture them in their lounge room, at the swimming pool, with friends, reading, and so on.

Now, with all of these images in your mind, start to think about different things that this person could use in their daily routine. When you picture their work desk, think about pens, paper, flowers, pictures, picture frames, a bag, a wallet, and so on. Picture yourself looking around their desk for clues for presents. Do the same thing with their home and their clothes. Look and listen for details, colours, sizes, sounds, textures, signs and comments. Don't limit yourself to just what you can see. You should also hear sounds, people's comments and what you would be saying to yourself, and think about how you feel, how others feel, what it feels like to touch something. Use all of your senses to take you to that place. You are a detective looking for clues. The scene is in your mind and you are looking around this landscape in your imagination for the clue to solve the mystery ... what would be a great present?

Visualisation is always my starting point when I am working on an idea, whether it is for business or something personal. I often combine a number of tools when designing ideas, and I have found that this tool is always one of the first that I call upon. In a business sense I use visualisation to see the product, company or service being used by the customer. I picture the customer, what's going on in their world, what they do, how they use the product. I picture them with the product and try to see, feel and hear what they do, looking for triggers to get the associations and freethinking started. Visualisation is a wonderful creative tool for you to try. No props are needed and it's so easy — you can do it right now.

This process also works extremely well for goal setting. Visualisation in this case is simply a method of helping to make your written dreams come to life. You must have a clear picture in your mind of what it is that you desire. For example, if you want to lose some weight then you would visualise yourself as having already lost the weight — see yourself healthy. You would see yourself enjoying life without that extra weight, you'd see all the things you would do, hear what people would be saying to you, look at what you would be wearing now and imagine how you would feel. Perhaps you want to visualise yourself running and finishing your first marathon, as I did. By visualising the whole experience I could see the whole race clearly in my mind — the start, the drink stations, the crowds, the pain, and most importantly the finish and the exact time that I was going to cross the line in. For four months prior to the race, I saw a vivid picture in my mind of the clock as I went across the finish line in the Olympic Stadium, and I beat my visualised time by three minutes. I truly believe that if I had not visualised and set written goals then I would have run a much slower race.

You must realise that visualisation alone won't get you there; you cannot simply visualise an outcome and then sit around waiting for it to happen. In the case of goal setting, creative visualisation helps to program your mind to the outcomes you have set. It is a very powerful tool, but you must be very clear about what it is that you are visualising, and you must have total commitment to it — don't try to do it half-heartedly.

I do have one word of advice regarding visualisation. Many people have become experts at visualising the wrong thing; that is, the wrong outcome. Through the language they use, their belief in themselves and the way they visualise, people can actually program themselves for less-than-favourable outcomes. You can visualise bad things equally as well as you can visualise good things, so be very careful in a performance sense not to visualise what you *don't* want to happen as opposed to what you *do* want to happen. The classic example of this is the guy who walks onto the golf course and tees up with a water hazard in front of him. He is completely focused on visualising, 'Don't hit it in the water, don't hit it in the water, don't hit it in the water.' Next thing you know … whack … plop! Where does the ball end up? Exactly where he saw it going — into the water! So always remember to visualise good things in a performance sense and not bad things, and when a bad image comes to mind, be sure to wipe it out and replace it with an image of a great thing.

I once used the visualisation technique with a workshop group, asking them to visualise their eightieth birthday party. I had them see the guests, experience the expressions on people's faces, and even hear the speeches. After the visualisation, I had the group write down what the guests had said during the speeches. We then had a few volunteers read out the speeches, and they were so moving at times that people had tears in their eyes as they read them out. Visualisation can be such a powerful tool that I have heard it said that during competition some gymnasts can visualise or imagine their routines so intensely that they perspire and raise their heart rate whilst sitting still!

Walt Disney died before the wonderful Walt Disney World in Florida opened its doors. I once read a story about Roy Disney, who was the brother of the incredibly creative Walt Disney. On the day that Walt Disney World was opened to the public in Florida, Roy was driving a journalist about the park in one of those little golf carts. The journalist turned to Roy and said, 'This is fantastic, it's a shame that Walt never saw it.' Roy just smiled at the journalist and said, 'Walt did see it, that's why you're seeing it today!'

See it then do it!

Recently whilst conducting a workshop on creative thinking in Sydney I met up with Wendy, who I had met a few years prior in another creative session that I had run in the Blue Mountains of New South Wales. We began discussing that previous workshop, and she mentioned that a number of the tools that we had discussed and used in that workshop were still being used by her company today and had in fact gone on to become an integral part of the culture of this organisation.

One particular tool that we discussed in the workshop that day was a visualisation called 'Put it in the balloon'. During the session I had all the participants lie on the floor with their eyes closed, I put on some relaxing music from Enya and had them take nice deep breaths to relax their minds and their bodies. Through the tone of my voice and the music I encouraged them to drift away from the room that we were working in to a relaxing place by the ocean. During this visualisation, the group was encouraged to see themselves walking along the shoreline where they come across a large hot-air balloon tethered to the beach. They were encouraged to take all their troubles and worries and put them into the balloon. Then they untie the balloon and watch it drift off into the sky, taking all their troubles and worries further and further away and leaving them in a trouble-free world in which to play.

The visualisation was a great success, and long after I had left it became a common saying around the office to 'put it in the balloon'. This occurred whenever people started listing problems or reasons why something could not happen, either in a meeting or a creative session or when a new idea was introduced and people would not give it a fair hearing. They were told to 'put it in the balloon' and let it go. I found it quite amusing and rewarding that the visualisation had such an impact, but it does go to show two things: firstly the power of visualisation, and secondly how things when they are taken and applied to the business can actually enhance and add to the culture of the organisation.

It is very gratifying as a presenter to hear that your material has become part of an organisation and that in some cases it has made a substantial contribution to the success or shape of a business, but in the end this book won't do the work for you. It comes down to the individuals and the company to take new learnings and do something with them. This group obviously decided that this concept worked really well for them, and it seems to be helping. They are one of Australia's foremost producers of health products and snacks, and seemingly they are going from strength to strength.

In summary, here are some things to consider when visualising ideas:

- Firstly, get relaxed. Breathe deeply, settle back and clear your mind.

■ Create an image in your mind of what it is that you are thinking about.

■ Let your mind wander like a detective looking for clues, but instead you are searching out ideas. Drift about the topic, looking for pieces to the idea.

■ Develop clear images of what it is you're visualising.

■ Give it time. Sometimes it may take a little while to create the image, but be assured it will happen.

Key 3: Smaller pieces

There is a saying, 'You can eat an elephant, you just have to take small bites', and the same logic applies to creativity. Sometimes when we are trying to find an answer to an issue or a problem, we tend to look at the whole problem and try to find one big idea or one big solution to encompass it all, which can sometimes be quite a task. Sometimes that is the most appropriate way for the issue to be tackled. However, there are also times when you should take a step back and ask what elements make up this issue. By using drawings or a flipchart you may be able to walk through the problems and identify the pieces that make up the task. You may even identify areas that were not obvious at all from the start, and by tackling those issues first you might be able to manage the whole problem. When you can see the problem broken down into smaller pieces, it also allows you to ask the question, 'What is really going on here, or what is the real issue?' It can offer you a clear or different perspective.

As an example, say we are putting together an event and we are looking for some new ideas. If we break it down into smaller pieces — the tickets, the invitations, the envelopes, the RSVP, the artwork, the texture, the venue, the times, the guest list, the parking, the car park, and so on — and think about each piece individually to see what we could do to make it special, don't you think we could do something really creative?

The concept of breaking things down into smaller pieces was one key on my creative key ring that I used frequently when I worked in the radio industry. Because I was working in the promotions area, we were responsible for working with the sales team to assist them in raising advertising revenue. The sales people would bring us a request from a client for a promotional activity, and if our idea was better than the idea from the other stations that we were competing with, then the client would spend their money with us. At times the other stations had more listeners than us, and so it was up to us to come up with the best idea that we could generate to woo the client to our station.

On one particular occasion, when we did have fewer listeners than our competitors, we were given a client request from a very large home electronics company. They made portable stereos and cassette players, and wanted an idea based around adventure and the outdoors. Now because we had fewer listeners, our ideas and everything that went with them had to be good. We looked at every part of the request to see what we could do better and differently to the opposition. Apart from the idea itself, we looked at where we would present the idea, how we would present it, how the client would get there, what they would do afterwards, we thought about sound, the follow-up after the presentation, and so it went. We ended up doing our presentation on the deck of a submarine in Sydney Harbour. We collected the client from their office in a giant double-decker bus that featured the radio station logo, and drove them to the SS Platypus Submarine Base where they boarded the sub. The presentation on the deck of the submarine took about forty-five minutes, and was followed by a tour of the sub given by the captain of the vessel. We then had lunch with the client in the officers' mess. You can imagine how impressed the client was, and yes we did win the client's business, which was worth quite a lot of money to the station.

On another occasion the idea was that two radio station listeners would win an adventure trip to Russia. The prize included shooting live rounds from a Blackhawk Chopper, a fly-by in a Russian Mig, and a ride in a Russian tank. It was a pretty cool prize, and thankfully the winner and the friend came home to Australia in one piece. It was a great example of how, when we broke things down into smaller pieces, we were able to add value at a number of different levels within the challenge. The radio station did not have the most listeners but we did have the best ideas, and quite often that was more than enough to win the day. We used the same creative process of breaking things into smaller pieces on numerous occasions with a variety of clients, and over time the station gained a reputation of fostering a really creative environment. To this day it still carries that reputation.

While we are on the topic of radio, I recently saw a documentary on the rock band Bon Jovi. Now Bon Jovi really are a bunch of guys who have reinvented themselves time and time again to remain at the top of the rock music industry. In an interview during the documentary, lead singer Jon Bon Jovi was asked how he and the other members of the band came up with their songs. He said that they first get the title for the song, then they get a feel for what it could be, then they start to write the music. It is not done in one sitting, but instead by breaking the song-writing process into small pieces which when assembled together form the great idea. As Jon Bon Jovi himself said during the interview, it is a process. They first come up with the title of the song, then the music, and then the lyrics. Breaking it down into smaller pieces can work no matter what the industry, community or area you are working with.

So next time you are faced with an opportunity to think up some creative new thoughts, try taking out a piece of paper and breaking the problem down into smaller pieces before you start your thinking process. Mind mapping can also be a great process for breaking the issue down into more manageable pieces. Once you have your list of pieces you can then start to develop ideas for each piece. You will be amazed at how this helps your thinking process.

Key 4: Brainwriting

Brainwriting is a non-verbal brainstorming technique that has proven very successful in smaller workshops of around five or six people. Here's how it works. Arrange the group on chairs or on the floor in a circle, facing the centre of the circle. When everybody is settled, give each person a clean piece of paper. At the top of that piece of paper they should each write the issue for which they will be collecting ideas. The issue should be framed in such a way as, 'In what ways could we …' Under the heading they are instructed to write down an idea in response to the question. Once everyone has completed this, they pass their page to the person immediately on their right and in turn they receive a page from the person on their left. They then look at the idea that was written down by the other person, and they can either add to that idea or write down a completely new idea under the previous one, and pass the page once again to the person on their right. The process continues until the page has gone full circle and returned to its person of origin. It shouldn't take long at all, and before you know it you have a whole list of ideas on the page in front of you.

Let's say the question is, 'In what ways could we improve our reception area?' Each person writes that down as the heading at the top of his or her page. Underneath that they write an idea or a way in which they could improve their reception area. Once everyone has written down an idea, they pass their page to the person on their immediate right. Consequently, the person who has just passed on the page will receive a different page from the person on their left. They then look at the idea that has been written down by the person on their left, and they can either add to that idea or perhaps think up a completely new idea. They write this idea on the same piece of paper under the first idea, so the piece of paper in front of them will now have a question at the top followed by two different ideas written underneath. Once again they pass the page to the person on their right, and at the same time receive another one from the person on their left. This process continues until the page has been right around the circle. If there are five people in the circle then when the page comes back it will have five different ideas on it, and in a very short period of time you would have collected 25 great ideas.

Now that you have all these pages of ideas, how do you decide which are the best? Each person reviews the list of ideas in front of them and puts a tick next to the idea that they like the best. The page is once again passed to the person on their right and they again receive a page from the person on their left, and so on. When your page finally returns to you, you should be able to circle the idea that has the most ticks; that is, the idea that was voted the best on the page by the group. At this point I would suggest you might like to put these top ideas up on a flipchart so that all the people in the group can see them. Once you have done that, you can run through the same process with the group to select the best idea, however use the board this time; that is, have each person in the group look at the board and put a tick against the idea they think is the strongest idea. Ultimately the group decides on the idea or the ideas that are strongest from the original list.

Brainwriting is quick, it is efficient and it is a terrific tool to use as a variation on brainstorming. Because it is non-verbal, it is also ideal to use if you have a group of people who are perhaps more concerned about speaking up in front of a group or who are a little hesitant in their approach to the brainstorming process.

Key 5: As if

The 'As if' tool is very valuable when problem-solving, and apparently Einstein himself used it a great deal to change his focus by drawing a metaphor for the problem; he would address the metaphor, which in turn took him towards his ultimate solution. Often changing your focus frees you up to be open and honest, and gives you previously unthought-of solutions to challenging situations or issues.

Here is an interesting example. I was once working at a four-day conference at a retreat in Australia. The client was a big entertainment company and they wanted some new, big, focused ideas for their company from the attending executives. The challenge was to get the ideas out of the executives, as in some environments the participants will not give their honest feedback for what could be a variety of reasons. For example, perhaps the boss is in the room, there is a negative 'shoot them down' mentality within the group, they don't practise PPC, or they are just not happy with the way things are going in the business. I was faced with one of these situations, so I tried something new in order to get some new and honest ideas out of the forty people in the room — I sacked them all!

Instead of having a room full of employed executives of the company, I asked them to instead become overpaid consultants to the company. In this role, I asked them to write down the wage they would like to be paid and then had them double it. I then asked them as a highly paid consultant to tell me what they would do in the next twelve months to make a quantum leap forward in the business. They were to be honest as a consultant, and any changes that they would make would be considered. As they were now consultants and not employees, they found they could afford to be brutally honest, and it worked wonders. We spent the day going through the consultants' ideas and setting strategies in place to make the best ideas happen. The team took on the roles so passionately, I even heard one of the higher level executives of the company — acting as a consultant — tell one of his fellow consultants to add in some graphics to their ideas as 'we can charge more for that!'

In the case of the entertainment company, I changed their focus by making them consultants, which meant that it was not *their* opinion, it was the opinion of consultants that they were giving, and it freed them up to be open and honest in a way that they felt they could not have been otherwise. It is such a simple tool, and one that you may wish to use from time to time either for yourself or when working with a team.

Address a problem as if you are consultants, or as if you could not lose, or as if you owned the business, or as if you were Walt Disney or Bill Gates. You will be surprised at how it can change the way of thinking, and at the results that you will achieve!

Key 6: The power of questions

I believe that one of the secrets to creativity and free-thinking is questioning. If we were to simply ask more and better questions, I believe that the number of new ideas and innovations would increase dramatically. How often do you see a new product or idea and think to yourself, 'That's so obvious, why did it take so long for this to come about?' Quite often it is because no-one asked the following questions: What if? Why not? What else? It is questions such as these that create options and start the creative ball rolling.

Here is a fun exercise for you to do in your own time. When you next engage in a conversation with someone or you are part of a conversation between a number of people, step back and take note of how many questions are asked during the conversation as opposed to how many statements are made. You may or may not be surprised to realise that most people speak in statements and ask questions infrequently; they prefer to share information with each other rather than ask questions. And this often reflects the fact that people are also not listening; when other people are talking they aren't listening, they are just waiting for their turn to talk again! It's a fascinating exercise, and I mention it to make you aware of how little we use the art of questioning.

Most of the great breakthroughs and discoveries in our past began with simple questions such as: How? What's another way? What if? Why not? How could we? What else could we do? In order to find new opportunities, we must be constantly asking questions of ourselves.

I have made a point of including more questions in my own interactions, and I play with this at parties and functions or when I am likely to find myself with strangers. I consciously ask question after question, not just to get to know this person but more importantly to train myself to constantly dig for the next question.

In 1997 I attended the Creative Problem Solving Institute in Buffalo NY, and one of the workshops I attended was run by Jack Wolf from a Florida-based company called Lifelong Learning Partners. During the class, Jack introduced me to a simple but very effective technique called 'What Questions'. When he first told me about What Questions, I actually said to myself, 'Come on Jack, it can't be that simple', but it was!

'What Questions' are based on a simple premise: rather that asking an individual or a group for a single answer, you instead ask them for 'what three things?' For example, rather than asking someone, 'What would you like for your birthday?', you would ask, 'What three things would you like for your birthday?'

Since Jack introduced me to What Questions, I have used it extensively as it is such a successful tool for idea generation. Generally speaking, when you ask people to answer a single question they can usually give you an answer off the top of their head without giving the question a great deal of thought. If, however, you ask them 'what three things', it makes them think a bit more before answering. This is the secret to the technique — allowing people the time and opportunity to think about their answer and to ponder the question to find three things, and more often than not it is the third thing that they come up with that is the best idea of all! It's just that they never had much inclination to think about 'what else?' (It is important to note at this point that three seems to be the magic number for the 'what' questions. If you ask for 'what two things', answers still tend to come fairly easily without too much thought, and if you ask for four or five things it becomes too hard and people don't want to play.) You can use this fantastic technique equally successfully in a business environment or at home. I also use it when taking a brief from a client for a job. I will ask them what three things they would like to have the participants achieve when they walk out of the room at the end of the day. The first two are easy, and then I keep pushing for the third.

I saw an interesting story recently in a local Sydney newspaper about young author Matthew Reilly, who has an Australian bestseller and has just signed publishing deals in the USA and Europe. He's also doing a television series and writing a screenplay. The journalist writing the article asked Matthew how it all started, and he replied that it all started with the simple question, 'What if?' He develops his stories by using the what if technique: What if I could do this? What if that happened? What if we did not do that, what would happen? And so on. At one point early on, without a publisher, he asked himself, 'What if I published it myself?' He borrowed $5000, published himself, and the rest is history.[10]

Here is yet another example of the power of 'what if': I was sitting at a table with the general manager of

---

10   *The Mosman Daily*, Thursday 7 October 1999, p1.

a field marketing company during the lunch break of a workshop in northern New South Wales when out of the blue she said to me, 'Wouldn't it be great if we didn't have demonstrators?' Now amongst other services, this company provided their clients with outsourced staff who would visit supermarkets and offer shoppers samples of products their clients were selling. They might offer you a sample of a piece of chocolate, a new yoghurt or maybe a barbecue sausage. These people are referred to as demonstrators or sampling staff. The company had recently been experiencing all sorts of issues with their demonstrators, and the people within the organisation had developed a negative association to the field staff.

With this in mind, I said to Simone, 'What if you didn't have any demonstrators at all?' After the laughter had died down at the table, I said it again, 'No think about it, what if you didn't have any demonstrators?' Now everyone at the table had stopped eating and was looking at me as if to say, 'How did you get this job, what was in your tuna salad, and are you kidding?' I asked them to consider the question. Given the fact that they were doing some work in the redirection of the company, what if they were to no longer have demonstrators, but instead had a team of people in the field with a different name, a name that their company could own, a name that had a good feeling about it and a name that people were proud to be associated with. All of the negative perceptions carried with the name 'demonstrators' would be lost, and there could be a new start. It would also position the staff of this company above those of the opposition who were still just demonstrators. It also reinforced the fact that the staff in the field are in fact marketing the clients' products face to face with the customers, making them an important cog in the machine. With renewed enthusiasm, tools and procedures, maybe they and the management would have a new attitude to their role.

Well, it worked. That afternoon, Simone and her team went about putting in place the first steps to re-branding their field staff. They set down a new plan for the future that involved extensive training for the field teams, new uniforms, new accountability procedures and in general giving the teams a new sense of direction and purpose. Some time later, I am delighted to say that their business has exploded and they are the market leaders in their field in Australia. They are setting the pace with regards to field marketing staff, with their field marketing representatives having new uniforms, new procedures, a new name, a full training program and a new attitude. Staff turnover has also dropped dramatically. And to think it all started with a simple question … what if?

In their book *A Crash Course in Creativity*, Brian Clegg and Paul Birch have an interesting exercise. They break a workshop of participants into groups, and ask each group in the room to list all of the uses for a coat hanger. Once that has been done, they then ask the groups to list all of the things that you can't do with a coat hanger. From experience I can say that the can't list is usually longer than the can list. Once completed, they then ask the groups to go through the can't list and challenge each item to see whether, in fact, they could move tho can't into the can list. For example, you can't eat a coat hanger ... what if you could? What if it was made of liquorice — we did not say what the coat hanger was made of (most assume it is a metal coat hanger). You can't drink it; what if it was made of — you guessed it — ice!

Then you get the usual reply ... 'Oh, you can't have sex with a coat hanger.' Well, what if you met a person who hangs coats in a restaurant for a living, and you took them home! They are a coat hanger! What I like most about this exercise is that people automatically assume the coat hanger is made of a certain material and immediately build parameters around what it can and can't do. The ideas that will take you and the company you work for forward are the ones that get away from the normal way of doing things and say, what if? What if it was made of lollies, what if you could drive it, what would it be then? How could you fly a coat hanger to the moon? Suddenly you have fewer barriers and less restrictions, and it opens you up to a whole word of possibilities!

I get excited in workshops when I challenge a group and say, what if you did do this? What if it was not like that ... what if? Once the team get their heads around a different way of thinking, they then become charged up by the endless possibilities. The limit then is only your imagination. Of course when I first do it, I get looked at like I have two heads, but I can live with that! Actually, what if I did have two heads ...

Another great example of this occurred when I was working with an executive team at a retreat over three days. On the final day, we were doing an exercise based

BLOTCH

CRIGHS

BLUKYC

The Vault, The Entertainment Quarter, Moore Park, NSW

Ask Einstein™ **Ask Einstein™**

www.bluemooncreative.com.au   www.bluemooncreative.com.au

Ask Einstein™ **Ask Einstein™**

www.bluemooncreative.com.au   www.bluemooncreative.com.au

Ask Einstein™ **Ask Einstein™**

www.bluemooncreative.com.au   www.bluemooncreative.com.au

Ask Einstein Cards (front)

Imagine if
it was illogical

Imagine if
you had more
money

Imagine if
there was more
of it

Imagine if
it was practical

Imagine if
you could create
a new logo

Imagine if
you could delete
hierarchy

Imagine if
you could
outsource it

Imagine if
you could change
the logo

Imagine if
you could add
hierarchy

Imagine if
you had less
money

Imagine if
you could change
the shape

Imagine if
it was less
corporate

Imagine if
it was more
corporate

Imagine if
you could change
its culture

Imagine if
you could take it
overseas

Ask Einstein Cards (back)

The Spin Cycle

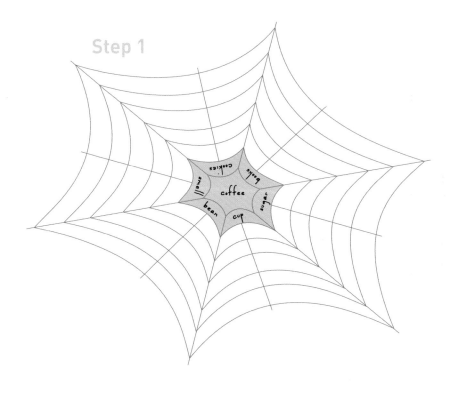

The Spider's Web

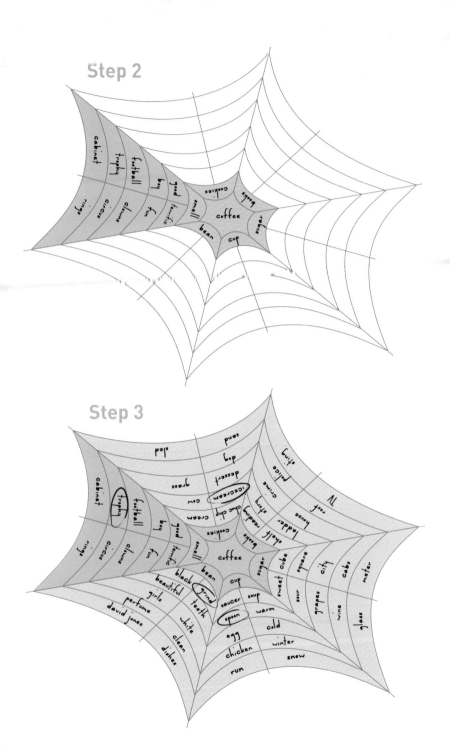

Step 2

Step 3

on breakthrough thinking. They really wanted to challenge their business to find new and exciting ways to do things. I started the sessions with the 'what ifs', giving an example of breakthrough thinking by suggesting they sack the CEO (he was in the room). Once the roar of laughter died down, I explained that it might be something to consider ... what if they did? Anyway, the teams then split into groups and disappeared into different areas of the retreat. On returning to the conference room some sixty minutes later, the groups decided that one of the ideas they would pursue would be the sacking of the CEO. Why? They believed that they needed to set up a more efficient system for succession planning for when the CEO eventually stepped aside. They also wanted him to spend less time in the business and more time working on the business. This was a major change in thinking for the team, and it came from something that at first seemed outrageous but when they really thought it through it was a key factor for the business going forward. They came up with three other breakthrough ideas in the same vein.

Try challenging how you do things. Try breaking the business or your own life into smaller chunks and then challenge everything. What if we did not live here? What if I did not go to the office every day? What if the clients came to me? What if the colour of our cola was not brown but yellow? What if their football jumper was not red and white, but our company colours ... what if, what if, what if ... Challenge the most unchallengeable ... slay the sacred cow. Now you may not take up every idea, but if you take up one in fifty, what could that one idea be worth? True idea generation is about building lists of options. By challenging the unchallengeable, you are truly getting to the ideas that are ground-breaking, and what's more, it is the fun and exciting part of idea generation and freethinking.

The same thing can be done with 'why' questions. The Japanese suggest you ask the 'why' question five times to truly understand a situation or a problem. Take this as an example: imagine that a worker was injured using a machine in a factory. Rather than say that perhaps it was just an unfortunate mishap, the first step would be to ask *why*. Perhaps it was because a strap from his overalls became caught in the machine. Why? Because it was hanging loose. Why? Because it had not been repaired by the service department when requested. Why? Because they had not processed his request for repairs. Why? Because they are understaffed and cannot keep up with the repairs as they are requested. So the real issue then is with the staffing of the service department and not the machine itself or an operator error. A problem well stated is a problem half solved, so use questions to get to the root cause of issues.

Once you have asked the questions 'what if' and 'why', and you have found an interesting idea to probe, you can then go about framing the same question as: In what ways could we make that happen? The 'what if' or 'why' questions probe the new thinking, and once done we then need to move on and find ways of making it happen; that is, what do we need to do to bring our idea to life? As you can see, it all centres on curiosity and questions, questions and more questions!

Key 7: Listen to this

In addition to my belief in the power of questions, I am also a great believer in the power of listening. Although there is a lot written and said about listening, I still find it fascinating that most people have such a lack of understanding about what it takes to really listen well. Training programs, audio tapes, books, lectures and even television programs spruik the secrets of listening effectively, but in fact it's not that hard to be a good listener. In fact anyone can improve his or her listening skills with a little effort, but it is surprising how few people do. If only they knew how powerful being a good listener is, I am sure it would change their approach to conversations and discussions.

Listening can be used very effectively as a creative tool. Someone who uses listening very successfully as a creative medium is US talk show host David Letterman. One of his great skills is his ability to 'hook' one question out of another, and he uses it to great effect when interviewing his guests on the show. What I mean by this is that when Dave asks a question he really listens to the answer, and he uses a piece of the answer as a hook to his next question. Here's an example of what I mean in an interview situation:

Dave: 'So, Jack, what have you been doing this summer?'

Jack: 'I went up to my holiday home in Colorado.'

Dave: 'What sort of things do you do up there in Colorado?'

Jack: 'Mostly skiing and snowboarding.'

Dave: 'So are you a good snowboarder?'

Jack: 'No, I'm actually just learning how to do it.'

Dave: 'So, is it a hard thing to learn how to snowboard?'

And so on ...

As you can see, Dave listens to what is said by his guest and then simply finds something interesting in the answer to act as a hook to the next question. Hooking is a simple and easy-to-use tip to improve your listening skills.

Remember people love to chat, and you will probably find that people will enjoy speaking with you because they feel as though you really *do* listen. Generally when in a conversation you will find that people tend to exchange statements as opposed to questions, and that people are talking *at* each other, never really taking the time to consider what the other person has said and whether there is real interest in what they have said; they are sitting there waiting for their turn to speak. Some do not even wait for the other person to finish before they start to speak.

Your new listening skills are sure to draw out some very interesting conversations with your partner, friends and colleagues, and the hooking process will have people recognising you as a good listener, an interesting person to talk to, and, who knows, maybe even a potential talk show host!

Do we really listen?

Do you really listen when you are engaged in a conversation? You might say that of course you do, but if you think about it, do you really? Before you can use listening as a creative tool, it might be worth taking a moment to consider this question.

I was working out at the gym last week when I noticed a young guy making his way onto a running machine. He set the presets to a slow walk, and once the platform started to move he immediately picked up his mobile phone to make a call. For twenty minutes he continued to slowly walk on the machine whilst chatting on the phone. Now I have to ask you whether he could possibly be fully engaged in either of the activities he was doing. You would have to say no, although he may beg to differ. Not only was he wasting his precious time on the running machine, he was also far from giving the person on the other end of the line his full attention.

When I turned my attention away from the guy on the treadmill, I saw out the window a young lady out on her balcony speaking on the telephone with a weeding tool in her hand, weeding the small garden on the balcony. She also managed to pick up some odds and ends on the balcony, rearrange the furniture and paint her toenails, all in the space of the fifteen-minute telephone conversation. Once again I question whether she could possibly be completely engaged in either of the occupations she undertook during that time. My suggestion would be no (despite being told often that women can multi-task much more effectively than men!).

When you do engage in a conversation either face to face or down the telephone line, the most powerful thing you can do for the other person is to give them your full attention. Thinking back to the story of the Buddhist monk that I mentioned earlier in the book, if you truly want to do something properly then when you hold a conversation with someone you should just listen, or just talk; don't also try to exercise, eat, read a magazine, do the housework or, worse yet, talk with someone else. Really listening means being fully focused on the person you are conversing with — focused on their words, tone, body language (if you can see them) and feelings, and this is very difficult to achieve when you are engaged in any other activity (or two), no matter how simple. I think everyone can relate to sitting at a desk deep in conversation on the telephone, whilst checking emails, flicking through a magazine and eating a snack on the run, the result of which is that we are really not doing anything well, and worse still our minds are so busy we cannot think clearly let alone creatively about what is being said to us, or what we are trying to read, eat and do at the same time. So the next time you are tempted to make use of the time you are spending on the phone by doing something else, take a moment and think if that is really what you want to do.

Key 8: Ask Einstein

There is no doubt that the right questions can not only stimulate your thinking, but also create new angles that you may not have considered previously. Blue Moon has developed a creative tool called Ask Einstein that allows the participants of any creative session to apply hundreds of unique directional questions to find innovative solutions to challenges and opportunities.

No matter how large the group, or what the issues may be, the unique Ask Einstein card questions allow groups and individuals to unlock their great ideas. Creativity is all about stimulating your mind, and this fun, interactive tool will do exactly that. If you don't have access to the Ask Einstein cards, you can easily create your own by bundling together a range of different questions that will take your mind on interesting angles as you approach your problem or challenge. What I have found, though, is that people like to have a physical tool that they can pull out of their desk to apply to a problem; hence our card set was created. I have used the cards with great success around the world, and it never ceases to amaze me what fantastic ideas result from minds being stimulated in ways that are a little bit different to the norm.

Albert Einstein was a true believer in the application of questions to the problem-solving process, so to find your next 'wow' idea, just ask Einstein! In the colour section is a sample of what the Ask Einstein cards look like. Below is a list of some of the types of questions that the cards can pose to you in your creative sessions, and

117

a number of examples that illustrate how they may be used. Here are some sample Ask Einstein questions:

- Imagine if it was chocolate …

- Imagine if it was on the moon …

- Imagine if it was an ice cream …

- Imagine if it was in *The Sound of Music* …

- Imagine if it was a fairy tale …

- Imagine if it was hip hop …

- Imagine if it was a television show …

- Imagine if it was Armani …

When you turn over the card, ask yourself and/or the group: What does the question make you think of? What images can you see or hear? How can they be applied to our problem or creative issue? The cards are there to stimulate your mind to look at the topic under discussion from different and often unique perspectives, by giving you something to hang your thoughts and ideas on. The cards will sometimes — in fact almost always — be totally unrelated to your issue, and in most cases they will seem a little silly or even a little obscure … which is great. The obscurity of the questions steers your mind away from its well-trodden, traditional, logical and left-brained approach to the topic under discussion to places it would not normally ever think of going. It can result in a new angle or approach, a new direction to consider, or a new possibility that previously may not have seemed relevant. Get out of your old habits and send your mind on a voyage of exploration! I find that individuals and groups can often spend fifteen to twenty minutes on a single card alone once the creative angles start to present themselves.

Let's see how Ask Einstein might work for a coffee shop. We are searching for ways to stimulate sales in our fictitious coffee shop …

Let's say the first card you pick from your Ask Einstein pack (and the first question you ask yourself) is, 'What if it was less expensive?' Can our coffee shop perhaps offer a Tuesday morning special, selling coffee at a cheaper price? Or perhaps between 3 pm and 4 pm every afternoon in our quiet time we could sell take-away coffees for only $1 each?

The next card you pull out says, 'What if it was McDonald's?' Could the shop perhaps offer a drive-through service in which people can call ahead and we can have their takeaway coffee ready and run it outside to them in their car for $2 (one gold coin for ease of change)? Or could we organise a special express lane at the counter for those people who just want to order coffees, and once again sell the coffee for $2 in order to make it quick with limited change requirements?

The next card you pull out asks, 'What if it was a fairy tale?' Could we perhaps organise to have storybooks for kids available in the store so they can read them while mum has coffee? Or maybe design a fairy tale story and colouring-in book centred on the coffee shop that they are sitting in? Perhaps we could even have a large mega-sized cup of coffee based on the principles of the tea party in *Alice in Wonderland*? Another idea could be to introduce a special range of cups that are designed for kids, so that each cup has its own fairy tale character on it and the children can select the fairy tale cup they would like to have their hot milk or Milo served in, while mum and dad have their coffees.

As you can see, after using just a couple of cards we have managed to generate well over half-a-dozen unique ideas in a very short period of time. Once again, if you don't have the cards you can simply use the same principles by thinking up your own questions and presenting them to yourself or the group one at a time. The process works just as well when working on business ideas as it does for designing a dinner party, choosing a present for someone or generating an idea for a school function or non-profit organisation. The secret is to ponder interesting questions that take your mind from the normal way of thinking. Using our fairy tale card as another example of how you can use the cards, when you think about a fairy tale you may start to consider characters, storylines, an introduction, the plot, good guys, baddies, the setting, the author, and so on. With this in mind, you may start to think about your issue, whatever it may be; for example, are we getting the whole story? Are we profiling our characters (our people)? Where are we in our story (growth of the company)? What would the likely end look like (our vision)? What are the baddies likely to do (our competitors)? Do we have a plot (a plan)?

In a creative session I often use the Ask Einstein cards as just one of many possible tools to stimulate ideas and creative thinking. Some groups respond better to the cards than visualisation and vice versa, and often it is nice to break up the creative session by using a couple of tools rather than just sticking to one process. For example, you could use a couple of the Ask Einstein cards, draw up a Spider Web of associations, visualise your topic, and maybe run a forced connection activity (see below). Whatever combination of tools you may choose, remember that these tools work just as well for a group as they do if you are sitting by yourself and pondering ideas, so please give them a try and see what works for you.

> *'I have no special gift. I am only passionately curious.'*
> Albert Einstein[11]

Make your own set of cards, or contact us. Full packs of 150 Ask Einstein cards are available from Blue Moon Creative (see back of the book for details).

Key 9: Forced connections

Most people or organisations are looking for that unique idea that will stand out from all the others. Traditional brainstorming if done effectively can certainly generate loads of ideas, but when you are after that really unusual idea that makes people say, 'How did you think of that?', there is one tool in particular that I love to use and it is called Forced Connections.

Have you ever been shopping in a grocery store when an amazing idea just pops into your head, even though you were not exactly sure how it got there? Perhaps you

---

11 *How to Think Like Einstein: Simple Ways to Break the Rules and Discover Your Hidden Genius* by Scott Thorpe, Sourcebooks, 2000.

were looking at the washing powder when you had an idea for a spring clean promotion for your car dealership. That is a perfect example of a forced connection — a tool that can be used to generate ideas or opportunities utilising objects that are totally unrelated. In this case you associated the washing powder with your own business that has nothing whatsoever to do with either washing or cleaning products. This tool can be particularly useful in brainstorming sessions when you have come to a standstill and the creative juices are just not flowing.

Forced connections can be initiated using toys, pictures or unrelated objects that have little or nothing to do with the issue at hand. Say for example that we are looking for ideas as to how to stage more interesting sales meetings, but we are momentarily stuck for ideas. Look around you and see what you can use — perhaps it is as simple as a bowl of mints that is sitting right there on the table. Utilising a bowl of mints, how can we generate ideas as to what that more interesting sales meeting might look like? Your ideas might flow something like this:

- Because there is a plate of mints, everyone has to bring a plate of food to the next meeting.

- People always have lollies at the movies, so perhaps we can take the group to the movies and have our meeting after the movie to brainstorm ideas of how the movie might apply to our business.

- Because mints are cool and white, we give away a trip to the snow as a prize for the most innovative idea that is generated for the next sales meeting.

- Mint is also a plant, so we have our meeting in the botanic gardens.

- Mint is a lolly, so we invite someone from Darrell Lea chocolates to come along as a guest presenter at the next sales meeting to give us an idea as to how they market themselves and run their sales operations.

- Because there are so many mints in a bowl, each person has to bring a small piece of new information regarding our market to the next meeting.

- Mints are white, so we are going to have a white-themed sales meeting. We will also begin our meetings with what is 'white' about what we are doing and not what is 'wrong'! Okay, that may be going a bit far …

- Mints are round, so let's have a round-table topic of the day.

As you can see, you can use something that is totally unrelated to a normal opportunity or problem to generate and stimulate new ideas and ways of doing things! I have come across people who have had their sales meeting sitting under the Sydney Harbour Bridge and used the Harbour Bridge, the harbour, boats, the trains, children and the Opera House to generate ideas for their meeting. I know of another fantastic idea that was generated using frisbees and bowls of fruit. The stimulant can be almost anything, so long as it forces a connection between what you have and the idea that you are brainstorming — it is purely there as a stimulant and a starting point.

To really develop those unusual ideas, try using unrelated items and forcing a connection between the challenge at hand and the product you have selected. It is not a normal process of thinking and can take a little getting used to, but if you persist and get the hang of it, it can be an enormously valuable tool on your key ring. It is all about surrounding you and your creative team with stimulants that can take the brain where it would not normally go to force new connections. Our brain is so used to being taken down the same single pathway through habit. We need to find ways of introducing new and exciting pathways to lead us to the discovery of fresh ideas.

Forced connections can be used even when you are sitting at your own desk. When searching for ideas to solve a particular problem, take a look at those things sitting on your desk and see how they might relate to the challenge; for example, pens, papers, photos, plants, telephones, lamps, computers and disks. You might also decide to surround your desk with interesting items that you can grab at any time to force a connection for an idea. Toys, pictures, food, stationery products, newspapers and magazines can all assist in taking your mind to places that it would not naturally have gone. That is what forcing a connection is all about. This is how the *wow* ideas are designed. Ask the questions, 'What could we do with a … ', and, 'What else could we do?' Or, 'What does this make me think of … ?' I know of a stockbroking firm in Sydney that has whole floors themed around a topic.

One floor is the beach, another is the city, another is the town square, and yet another the country. When staff move departments, they move not only to a different floor but often also from the city to the country.

I generally use grocery items for my Forced Connection sessions. In fact, at Blue Moon's own workshop venue at the Entertainment Quarter in Sydney we have built our own supermarket in one of the breakout rooms for that very reason. Initially I will define the problem or challenge for the session, and then I send the participants into the supermarket to grab a few random items. We then use those items as the basis for the creative session. We recently had a session for a client and were faced with the prospect of coming up with interesting ideas to promote the vegetable artichoke, which I would have to say seemed rather challenging. Even though we had some very talented copywriters and promotions people in the room, I once again sent them into the supermarket to come back with a variety of unrelated items to use for forced connections. Within twenty minutes they had some extraordinary ideas that would never come about through the normal process of brainstorming or group discussion, and it was all through the use of forced connections.

On another occasion I was working with a group on the Gold Coast in Queensland when one of the people in the room wrote on the whiteboard in permanent ink … it happens! Well, we tried everything to get it off the board but it was stuck there good and proper. We wrote over it with removable pens (that usually works), tried that spray they provide, and even tried to use good old elbow grease, all to no avail. We had to keep the session moving, so we left it there and moved onto the next part of the workshop. About twenty minutes later, and in the middle of a discussion, the CEO of the business suddenly stood up, walked over to a bowl of fruit I had to the side of the room, grabbed a piece of pineapple, and started wiping the whiteboard with it! Lo and behold, the permanent ink came off … easily!

Of course everyone cheered, and me … I just wanted to know what made him think of that. He said that there had to be a way of getting it off, and that he looked around the room, saw the pineapple slice, and thought: it's acid, why not try that? That persistence, determination, curiosity and experimentation is what makes him a great leader. It is also a great example of Forced Connection in action. I would never have imagined using pineapple to remove the pen from the board, and certainly no-one else in the room had considered it as pineapple was totally unrelated to the problem at hand, but it worked and was a perfect example of what I had been talking about; as the name suggests, it involved forcing a connection between two unrelated items to design an idea or solution.

In another session, I was facilitating the creation of some sales promotional ideas for a company who was pitching for the work of a big coffee company. Initially the session was to take place in the client's boardroom (it happens too frequently). I asked them whether they were open to other suggestions, and thankfully they said they were — great! Initially I took the team of eight to a nearby supermarket and just had them wander the aisles, writing down notes on textures, flavours, unusual associations and other products that fitted with coffee, such as biscuits, milk, snacks and chocolate. We then drove to the centre of the city and sat outside a Starbucks coffee shop. Each person at the table had to order a different coffee — small, large, cream, no cream, decaf, half caff, syrup, no syrup, and so on.

When we all had a coffee, sugars, stirrers, waters, mugs and napkins, we started our session. I took out a roll of flipchart paper and some pens that I had brought along, and we began the process of using all of the notes from the supermarket, the coffees in front of us, the coffee accessories and our surrounds to come up with ideas. After we had spent a significant amount of time on the stimulants around us, I took the group across the road to a park where we lay on the ground observing the people around us, and once again we dreamed up ideas. The process took about three hours all up, and the group generated twelve flipchart pages full of ideas, and I don't have large handwriting! It was an extremely productive session, and they won the coffee business. This was yet another example of using forced connections using related and unrelated items in an environment that was conducive to creative thinking to successfully address the challenge at hand.

I once heard a story that Brian Wilson from the Beach Boys used to fill the recording studio with sand when writing their music. It must have worked for the band, because they have sold a lot of music. It is a very good idea to always have the product that you are creating ideas for in the session with you. Those products can be the actual product, other related or unrelated items or even a competitor's product like those used in my coffee example. Things that add colour that people can touch, feel, look at, and play with. This is just as important when you are working on your own.

When running a session or thinking on my own, I will quite often combine a number of different keys to achieve my desired outcome. Once I have determined the real issue, I may break things into smaller pieces and then use the forced connection method as one of the stimulants. Don't forget that the keys in this book should be mixed and matched as you see fit, so that they work for you. Alternately you may find that they work best in isolation. Either way, they are there to unlock your great ideas, so go out and get your brain some exercise!

Key 10: Brainstorming

Unlike a number of the more abstract tools I have outlined in this book, the use of brainstorming as a technique for generating ideas is something that most people have heard of, even if they're not exactly sure how it works. The inventors of the brainstorming process are Alex Osborne and Sid Parnes, who wrote the book *Applied Imagination*. This section of the chapter is devoted exclusively to their process — how brainstorming works, tips and tools for setting up the room, how to work successfully with attendees, and how to brainstorm effectively to ensure that you get the most out of your session. It is such a valuable and successful tool for generating ideas that it deserves to have some significant time spent on it to ensure that it is being carried out properly and will result in great ideas that you have come to expect from such a session.

In the hope of ensuring that the process is undertaken as Osborne and Parnes would have wished, I have devised an easy-to-remember acronym called the Creative Dancea to help simplify the process. I will go through each of the steps of the Creative Dancea shortly, but first I would like to discuss setting up the brainstorm.

How to brainstorm effectively: the set-up

First things first — before launching into any brainstorm session it is important to address the set-up of the session. I am often asked what the ideal number of people is to have in a brainstorming session, and there are a variety of different opinions as to that number. In my own personal view, I would suggest that a group of between six and eight people is a good number of people to work with. Anything fewer than five people and the group is getting rather small, and if there is any more than about twelve people in a group it can become a little hard to control if you are not used to running a session. Eight people is a great size; it is very manageable and it provides for good interaction yet it still allows for the group to divide into smaller breakout groups should you decide to do this. When deciding who should attend, I like to look to those people who have an open mind, are keen contributors, like to be challenged and like to take a different approach to tasks. It's not to say that everyone is not welcome in the brainstorm, but try to ensure that you also have a good selection of people with the sorts of qualities I have listed above, to get the most out of the session.

The next thing to consider is the location of your brainstorm. A large number of brainstorms inevitably end up taking place in a large office or boardroom, and that is fine, however if you have the opportunity I would strongly suggest that you get out of the boardroom, away from that big boardroom table and try to find somewhere a bit more creative and stimulating. I have done literally hundreds of sessions both inside offices and away from the office environment, and I can assure you that the degree of creativity and freethinking is so very much higher when the participants are away from the office and those boardroom tables which seem to suck the creative spirit out of people!

Why not visit a park, stop off in a cinema foyer, a conference room at a hotel, a cafe, the zoo, a function room, or someone's house for a creative session; the important thing is to change the environment if at all possible. As I have mentioned previously, it stands to reason that when you are away from the office you are exposed to any number of triggers and stimulants that you just can't replicate in a boardroom, let alone the added benefit of avoiding the distraction of phones and interruptions from other staff in the office. Depending on what you are brainstorming, who the target is, what the issue is and what it relates to, you can choose an environment that either stimulates thinking about the target of the brainstorm or the environment in which you are brainstorming. I have spoken to people who have run their brainstorms sitting underneath a bridge by the river, in amusement parks, shopping centres and cafes. Say you were brainstorming for ideas for young women aged between sixteen and twenty-four years old. In this case you may choose to run your brainstorming session in a shopping centre or a mall. You might decide to do it in a cafe that overlooks a cosmetics area, or in a shopping strip somewhere in your city that attracts young ladies. Look for different environments that can stimulate your creative mind and generate much more interesting ideas. Push the boundaries of how you normally do things and conduct your brainstorms at interesting locations in or out of the office — stimulate your mind and get out and about!

Regardless of where you set up, there are a number of things that you should also keep in mind, such as comfort and the availability of water. In setting up your preferred environment, ensure that your participants are comfortable, there aren't any mints or other confectionery available, and that there is plenty of water available. Dehydration will stifle your creativity, so endeavour to make plenty of water available so that people can refresh themselves. Please also ensure that people are comfortable where they are sitting, that they aren't too hot or too cold, and that they feel comfortable with the fact that they are there. Encourage people also to move around if they wish, as some people will become fidgety sitting in just one place, and these people tend to learn and think better if they are able to walk around the room or area. Don't be put off by this; these people are listening and paying as much attention as the others who are sitting down, it's just that this suits their preferred way of thinking and learning and they participate the best if this is allowed, and you should encourage that. If they aren't distracted or bored by the basics they can concentrate on generating great ideas. It is the small things that make all the difference! If people feel comfortable in their environment they will contribute to the brainstorm session. When facilitating a brainstorm, be sure to use eye contact, to welcome input from everybody in the room, and to encourage all of the people who are participating to come forward with ideas. Acknowledge ideas as they come forward and make people feel good about the fact that they have contributed something.

The other important thing you might want to think about with regards to your set-up is music. Select some appropriate music to play in the room to settle people as they walk in, or if you are in an environment outside of the work environment then perhaps take some music with you. Quite often creative sessions or brainstorms are occurring when people are coming from a working environment of telephones, meetings, back-to-back appointments, people coming in through their door at the same time that they are trying to get memos out. Sound familiar? I'm sure it does. Playing some relaxing Enya or some baroque music will calm them down from the day's activities, encouraging them to get into a nice relaxed state from when they walk into the room. If you can bring them to a point where their heart rate slows down to around sixty beats a minute they will feel a little less stressed and a bit more relaxed. A stressed environment will not promote creativity, it will stifle it, so even if they wonder what on earth is going on when they first walk into the room, it is an environment conducive to creative thinking and it will make a huge difference to the outcome of the session! When they are not thinking or are between sessions, play some current upbeat tracks that everyone will like, to get the heart rate going.

Lastly, here are a couple of little tips to help get those creative juices flowing. Certainly pictures of the product, consumer or issue that you are thinking about can be helpful if you are in a boardroom or an office situation and you don't have access to the environment and/ or consumer that you will be discussing. I've seen companies make up montages of the target for the product they will be discussing from magazines, and they have them framed and on the wall to stimulate discussion. The montage may have different photos of the audience they are appealing to, the food they eat, shots of where they go, the sport they play, their favourite heroes (music, sport or cultural heroes), perhaps even shots of the target in a social scene. All this information can be sourced easily from magazines.

Toys are also good fun to have around the room for people to play with, and they can also be valuable in stimulating good ideas. Funny glasses, balls to throw around, different-shaped building blocks, connect pens, play dough, lots of colour and movement is great in a room. If you want to do something different for your brainstorm, bring in a box of toys and let everybody play with them. Don't forget we are all kids at heart, and a big box of toys brings out the child within — everybody loves to play and be silly and this creates a very positive environment for your brainstorm. Toys take people away from their everyday environment, and this lets them know that they are there to create and do things differently. Yes, be prepared for some funny looks when people first see the toys and colour, but don't let the comments or funny looks concern you — once they get started and curiosity gets the better of them, people will start to play with the toys, and you'll find that they will quite enjoy the opportunity to be a kid. I have had some very funny experiences with people who have entered my room, thinking that what we were about to do was going to be silly and childish, but by the end of the session they are the same people asking me where I bought the toys!

If you would like to stimulate your sessions with toys, games, puzzles or more music for creativity, then I have found the most comprehensive and complete website is www.finkinc.com.au. The guys at FinkInc have done a wonderful job of putting together a collection of fun stuff to help you think, for your creative sessions with groups or individually when sitting at your desk. This is definitely a website worth checking out. They also carry our Blue Moon Creative 'Ask Einstein' cards and The Spider's Webs.

Remember if you are facilitating a group that your job is to facilitate; that is, to keep the group moving forward, to maintain control of the group and to provide as many stimulants as possible to generate pages of ideas.

Brainstorming guidelines

The next thing we are going to consider are some intellectual guidelines that you should set at the beginning of the session to ensure that everyone is moving in the right direction and that everybody knows the parameters of the session. It is important to note that they are *not* rules; they are just thoughts or guidelines for people to consider.

The first one is that there is no rank in the room. This means that for the duration of the brainstorm session, that may run from twenty minutes to an hour, everybody is on an equal pegging and there is no hierarchy in the room. There is no distinction between senior management and juniors — everybody in the room is equal and everybody's ideas have the same merit. This takes away the risks and the fear of participants that they may say something in front of the boss which may seem unacceptable or out of line. When management acknowledge this absence of rank in the room for the session it puts everyone at ease, and in this environment the group will want to contribute bigger and better ideas.

The second guideline is that combining ideas is great. If participants have hit a logjam in their flow of ideas and nothing is coming forth, they should be encouraged to look at other people's ideas and try to combine them to make a better idea.

Thirdly, I want everyone to know that silly is good. I want to encourage silly ideas and a bit of fun in the room. I really do want people to enjoy themselves, laugh, relax and have fun. Brainstorming should be an enjoyable process and wild, silly ideas are to be encouraged. When people say silly things it can often be a fantastic stepping stone for somebody else, and what could be a silly idea to one person may be the basis of a great idea to someone else.

Fourth, I also want people to piggyback ideas. Encourage the group to listen to the other participants in the room during the session and try to build on other people's suggestions. Often if people think about what someone else has said they can add to their ideas and develop new ones. This is also useful when you have temporarily run out of thoughts and you are looking for new stimulants.

My fifth guideline for the group is that the goal is a big long list of ideas. We want quantity, lots of ideas, so don't hold back, speak up and tell everyone all your ideas. Brainstorming is all about building lists no matter how silly some of those ideas may seem, or how left field they may be. I often find that some of the best and most innovative ideas come about after we have been brainstorming for quite some time. It is not until you have exhausted all of the left-brained, logical ideas that more right-brained, imaginative ideas come to the surface. Quite often it is the last third of ideas on your list from which will come the best ideas.

The sixth guideline I would like to give you has been mentioned earlier in the book, and that is that cheating is good, so give the group permission to cheat in the session. It's funny the reaction I get at the opening of a workshop when I encourage people to cheat.

They all put their hands over their mouths and snicker like they are naughty little kids. Now we are all taught at school not to cheat and we do carry that with us into our adult lives. I am not saying that anyone should cheat in the traditional sense of the word, but I do recommend cheating in the sense that it is okay to look at what other companies are doing, take their ideas and make them better. Cheating in this sense can also mean looking at the ideas of the person next to you in order to come up with an idea together that is better than just the idea they originally had. By putting on the board that it is okay to cheat in the session it means people feel free to have a bit of fun and freewheel, and it takes a bit of pressure off some individuals to have to come up with entirely original ideas. We all love to be naughty from time to time and everybody gets a kick out of the fact that the teacher is allowing people to cheat!

Finally, my last guideline is to defer judgment. Please ensure that everyone in the room is encouraged to defer judgment and not critique their own ideas or anyone else's before they have been put up on the board. Again, we are aiming for quantity not quality — the refining process can come much later down the line. Do not let that little voice in your head pre-judge any of your ideas so that you end up sharing only what you think are your best ideas — let the group decide that down the track. If someone comes up with an idea that you don't think will work that's okay, let them put their idea up on the board and if you have a different opinion then call out your idea and add it to the list also.

So in summary there should not be any rank in the room, everybody is equal. Combine ideas — look at what is already on the board and try to add bits to combine and make a better idea. Piggyback ideas — listen out for other people's ideas and try to find other ways to dovetail to add to the list and make it bigger. Go for quantity not quality. Go for lots of ideas rather than only the good ones as judged by that little voice in the back of your mind. Silly is great — we want the silly ideas. Feel free to have fun — enjoy the process. Come up with silly ideas because that could be a great stepping stone for somebody else. Lastly, defer judgment — hush that little voice inside your mind that says I won't say that because they will think I'm stupid, they will think it's a dumb idea or they will laugh at me or it will never work. Defer judgment — say it anyway!

By setting up some simple and straightforward guidelines for your brainstorm and by creating a comfortable and stimulating environment in which to work, you are off to a great start. The set-up, the environment, the guidelines and the way you run the brainstorm are just as important as the brainstorm itself, and yet they are so often overlooked in the rush to get the session underway. Next, I am going to discuss how to run the brainstorm itself in the most effective way possible.

Running the brainstorm session

Now that we have set the environment and the guidelines for the brainstorm, let's talk about the steps of the process itself. Most people that I speak to have heard of brainstorming and many have undertaken brainstorming sessions themselves, yet so few people fully understand the principles and brainstorm properly. In my experience, people tend to use brainstorming to generate lots of ideas but once the session is over the group disperses and the facilitator is left with pages of ideas and no way of deciding which ideas were good or otherwise and no commitment to using any of those ideas — they miss out on the vital evaluation stage of the process as outlined by Osborne and Parnes. So, in order to make the full brainstorming process more memorable, I have taken each of the steps and devised an easy-to-remember acronym to ensure that the brainstorm is undertaken properly — it is called the Creative Dancea.

The first <u>D</u> of Dancea is to determine the focus — wouldn't it be great if ...

The <u>A</u> is create some alternatives. This is your traditional brainstorm where you generate lots of ideas to solve the problem. The way to frame this is in what ways would we ...

<u>N</u> for is narrow down. Narrow it down to the best ideas by having all of the people in the room vote for which ideas they think are the best.

<u>C</u> is for criteria — once again make a list of all the criteria this idea must meet to be a successful idea. Narrow it down to the best ideas.

And <u>E</u> is evaluate your ideas with the success grid. Put your ideas down the side of a board or page, then go to your criteria and score them from one to five to work out which idea is the best idea.

And the final, but very important, step is the <u>A</u>ction plan.

Try this method and become a Creative Dancea. Below we will look at each of these steps individually.

Before starting a brainstorm, ensure everyone in the room is up to speed on the issue or product. It is best to do a short update for everybody in the room to have them understand any background information that may be pertinent to the brainstorm: why the brainstorm is taking place, what particular issues have brought you together, any internal projects, any environmental issues, any information that people should be aware of that may help inform them regarding the issue for the brainstorming.

D — Determine the issue

It's said that a problem well stated is a problem half solved. Often we begin brainstorming and problem-solving sessions without really knowing or understanding what the true issue under discussion actually is. So the first step is simply to determine the issue at hand, and the easiest and quickest way to do this is to ask the group the following question: wouldn't it be great if ... Identify the topic, and in an ideal world, if something was to occur with regards to that issue then wouldn't it be great if ... Throw it open for discussion and list all the different responses that you receive from the room. Once this has been achieved then you need to identify the person in the room who owns the issue and it is up to them to select from the list the most appropriate statement, or the one most suited to the brainstorm about to take place. Generally this is the person responsible for bringing the issue to the table in the first place or it's their responsibility within the organisation to find a solution to the issue or concern.

Say for example that the issue is that the kitchen at work is always dirty. Rather than ask the group to brainstorm ways in which to keep the kitchen clean, what you might do is ask the group, 'Wouldn't it be great if … ' You may then get responses such as:

- 'Wouldn't it be great if when you walk in the kitchen it was always tidy.'

- 'Wouldn't it be great if there were no dirty plates.'

- 'Wouldn't it be great if you could always find a fork to eat with.'

- 'Wouldn't it be great if there were no biscuit crumbs on the floor.'

- 'Wouldn't it be great if there were always biscuits in the kitchen'.

The person who owns the issue then goes through the list and identifies the core issue as, 'Wouldn't it be great if you walked into the kitchen and there were no dirty dishes.' So rather than brainstorming how to keep the kitchen clean, you are brainstorming ways to ensure that there are no dirty plates in the sink. Rather than the rather broad topic initially brought to the table, you have now determined a more specific topic that addresses the real nuts and bolts of the problem.

A — Alternatives

At this stage we want to generate as many alternatives as we can for our topic, which needs to be re-framed slightly for this stage of the discussion. If we have identified as our outcome that we would like to find ways in which to keep all the plates in the kitchen clean, then we need to re-frame the topic as follows: 'In what ways could we keep all the plates clean in the kitchen?'

With this question at the top of our page the aim here is to generate lots and lots of ideas to answer the question. We are looking for as many ideas as possible — hundreds of ideas if we can. The facilitator takes all those ideas and puts them up on a whiteboard or a flip-chart. So ideally at the end of the period of the brainstorm of fifteen or twenty minutes you will have all these ideas up on a board.

N — Narrow down the ideas

Now that we have all these ideas on the board or flip-chart, we need to narrow them down to those ideas that the room thinks are the best. The way to do this is with sticky dots that you buy from a stationery store, or if you don't have any coloured dots handy, you can just ask the participants to tick those ideas they like best. Each person in the room will be given a number of dots (you would normally allocate one dot for about every fifteen ideas you have up on the board, as a rough guide). Let's say we generated sixty ideas. Each person in the room would then receive four coloured dots. The group is then allocated three or four minutes, and during that time everyone is asked to place their sticky dots next to those ideas listed on the walls or boards that they think are the best to meet the required outcome; that is, place dots next to those ideas that you think will help keep the plates clean in the kitchen. If you really like one idea then you could put all four of your dots next to this idea. If you like two ideas you might put two dots on one and two dots on the other; it is up to you. Once that task has been completed, the facilitator goes back to the list of ideas to work out which three or four ideas received the most votes. You might want to put a circle around these ideas to highlight the ones that the *group* thought were the best ideas to meet the brief. At the end of this step, you should have somewhere between two and four ideas that are possible solutions to the challenge presented at the beginning of the session.

C — Criteria

In order to further identify the best idea from the ones you have just circled, the idea must meet certain success criteria as decided by the room; for example, if you were going to buy a brand new car then you have certain criteria in mind that the car must meet. I want it to be red, it must have four doors, it must have air conditioning and a CD player. If the car you select does not meet these criteria then you will not be happy with your purchase. The same logic applies to your list of possible solutions to the dirty kitchen. There are certain criteria your idea must meet in order for it to be the idea that you choose to run with.

To decide on the success criteria for your ideas, we need to have another little brainstorm session with the facilitator writing down as many suggestions as possible as to the criteria required to make these ideas successful. For our kitchen example, a list of possible success criteria might include the following: the plates in the kitchen must be cleaned, there must be plenty of plates to use in the kitchen at all times, it must be cost effective, it must be easy to implement, and it must be something that everybody agrees to. When we have once again come up with a list of ideas, we do the same thing as we did above — we allocate dots or ticks and again ask the group to mark those criteria that they think are the most important.

By the end of the criteria stage you should have narrowed the long list of ideas down to three or four of the best, and you also have three or four criteria by which to judge those ideas. Next we need to evaluate the ideas.

E — Evaluate

In order to evaluate our ideas against the criteria we have set down, we need to draw up a grid. Across the top of the grid we will list our criteria and down the side of the grid will be our three or four top ideas. At the point where the ideas meet the criteria, we rank each idea from one to five. If you give it a five it means the idea is absolutely spot on and nails the brief perfectly, and if you give it a one the idea doesn't meet the criteria at all. Going back to our kitchen example, one of the criteria might be that we always have clean plates in the kitchen, and one of the ideas might be that we purchase a dishwasher. In a score from one to five, you would think that the dishwasher idea would rank a five based on this criteria. However, it may not rank so highly on a cost criteria. At the end of the process you will have a total score for the dishwater idea together with a total score for the other top ideas.

The idea that has scored the highest against your criteria may be the idea that you choose to move forward with. It's important to note at this stage that just because a particular idea scores the highest doesn't mean that this will be the idea that you have to run with. You identify which criteria are most important and look at which ideas are going to meet your criteria, but remember you may have four or five other good ideas that you could choose to run with. Also, don't forget all those other ideas that you generated earlier in the session. If you wish, you can still put these ideas through the evaluation process at a later stage, so don't discard these ideas as not being of value.

A — Action plan

No brainstorm is truly complete without the action plan. The action plan moves the selected idea out of the realm of discussion and into reality. It is a plan outlining who is committing to do what and by when, in order to put the idea into motion. The real value of any brainstorm is in the outcome, and the real success comes when you do something with it. So please ensure that at the end of your brainstorm you commit to an action plan on paper and set it in motion, otherwise all that hard work can so easily go to waste!

So that's it — the Blue Moon Creative Dancea in all its glory. Here it is again as a quick summary:

The first step is Determining the focus (wouldn't it be great if …), then we generate some Alternatives (a long list of ideas). Next we Narrow down the list of ideas to the best three or four, as decided by the group as a whole (using spots or ticks), before deciding on the Criteria which the group thinks the idea needs to meet to be successful (another quick brainstorm). Finally, we Evaluate the ideas against the success criteria, and then formulate an Action plan to put the idea into action. It's as simple as that!

Why not try this method and become a Creative Dancea — you will be amazed at what you can come up with!

Key 11: The Spin Cycle

As I mentioned earlier, one of the most challenging tasks of the creative process is that of getting our minds to break free of their old habits and training them to approach problems or opportunities from different and unusual angles. This is particularly the case in established organisations or businesses of any type, whether they may be multi-million-dollar companies, small businesses or non-profit groups. Many organisations over time have created what we call 'sacred cows' within their culture. Sacred cows are those rules or parameters that have been established within an organisation such that those working in the business believe they could never challenge or change them. But it is only when we challenge and 'slay' these sacred cows that we really achieve breakthrough thinking.

The Spin Cycle (shown in the colour section in the middle of the book) is a creative tool I developed specifically to challenge these entrenched beliefs about an organisation or a product or service in a way that enables those involved to explore the possibilities without feeling uncomfortable. The tool has been designed as a pad, and lets users challenge the status quo by identifying and then slaying the sacred cows that have formed within their organisation. As with the Ask Einstein cards, I have developed the Spin Cycle tool into a physical item simply because I work with individuals and groups constantly and I have found that people like to use a creative tool that they can touch and see; they find it stimulating and they tend to use the technique more often as a result. However, please remember that you don't need the pad in order to use the principles effectively, and I am more than happy for you to draw up your own pads if you so wish.

The first step in using the Spin Cycle pad is to list down all the tangible attributes of whatever it is that you are discussing and place each one into one of the cows. If your business is a coffee shop then some of the attributes you might list could be:

■ We have cups.

■ We have sugar.

■ It is a place to relax.

- It sells coffee.

- The coffee is black.

- The coffee comes in a bean.

- The coffee shop has seats.

- The coffee shop has staff.

- The coffee shop serves cakes.

- The coffee shop has a coffee machine.

The next stage of the Spin Cycle is to take each one of these attributes and spin them around, looking for opposites or imagining a situation in which you may not have that attribute. For example, if a coffee shop always has chairs and tables then you may take that particular attribute. Start to consider the possibility of having a coffee shop without tables and chairs. What might that be like? Could it have long benches instead of chairs? Could it become a traditional Italian coffee bar with no seating at all, and people simply walk in, stand at the bar to drink their espresso, pay and then walk out? Perhaps you instead have round cocktail tables like you would see at a bar, and encourage people to stand around these bar tables and talk rather than sit down, or perhaps you could fit the coffee shop with couches or lilos that people can lay back on as opposed to having tables and chairs.

Another attribute noted on one of the cows was that your coffee shop sells cakes. By taking this attribute and 'spinning' it, you could consider posing the question, what if it didn't have cakes? What if your coffee shop only sold fresh, healthy food like vegetables with dips and salads? What if you had a charity supply and sell their cakes for you, or what if the coffee shop became more of a traditional espresso bar and you sold no food whatsoever but specialised in making excellent coffee? Or perhaps you don't sell cakes, only biscuits, so it becomes a coffee shop with a huge range of biscuits but no cakes.

Hopefully by now the concept behind the Spin Cycle is starting to become clear. By taking each of the tangible attributes of whatever it is you are thinking about and 'spinning' them, you begin to look for opposites, changes, additions and breakthroughs to change and slay the sacred cow. The types of questions you might want to ask are:

- What if it didn't have that?

- What if you couldn't do that?

- What if you did the opposite?

- What if you had less of it?

- What if it wasn't available?

- What if you didn't have one?

By asking these types of questions, you open the discussion up to new angles that would not have existed while the attributes were sacred cows.

Recently I was working with a group who were running a creative session for their client, a men's razor blade company. The aim of this particular session was to come up with ideas to launch a new men's blade. One of the tangible attributes that went into the Spin Cycle was that the blade was for men. Once they put the attribute of men into the Spin Cycle, they started thinking about, well what if the promotional activity wasn't targeted exclusively to men? What if we targeted the promotional activity also at women? This started a whole discussion based on the fact that razors are as appropriate for women as they are for men. The angle that they took was that a nice clean shave on a man is also great for women as they don't get razor burn or that harsh bristling effect when they are with their partner, so it is actually a huge advantage for women to have their men experience the closest shave possible, and if they want the closest shave they should buy the client's product. The group then proceeded to design a promotional campaign that enabled them to talk to women as well as to men.

A different group were running a similar exercise based on a client whose product was a breakfast cereal. One of the tangible attributes listed in that session was that breakfast cereal always comes in a box. During the session, they took the cereal box, spun it around and asked themselves, 'What if our breakfast cereal didn't come in a box?' The company decided to pursue the concept that their cereal should perhaps come in a plastic container that could then be used for other purposes in the kitchen or for kids to use as lunchboxes. Wouldn't you say this group was thinking differently about their product in ways that previously they wouldn't have considered?

For yet another group, one of the tangible attributes of their company was that there was always a CEO, so they took the CEO attribute and asked the question, 'What if we didn't have a CEO?' The group initially roared with laughter, but after they had settled down and really considered the question they thought it was in fact very relevant. On reflection, the group believed that there wasn't an effective succession plan in existence if their CEO ever did decide to leave the business, and that at the present time the CEO was working very much in the business as opposed to on the business. Pretending that they didn't have a CEO allowed the group to put in place a succession plan, new roles and job descriptions to be implemented, and the end result was that the CEO was able to work more on the direction the business was heading as opposed to the day-to-day running of the company. So yet again by taking what was previously a sacred cow within the business and putting it into the Spin Cycle, a couple of terrific ideas resulted that ended up making the day a great success for the individuals, the CEO and the business as a whole.

I recently spoke with a close associate of mine who has applied similar thinking to his own home. Instead of putting his new pool in the backyard as per usual, he had the pool installed on top of his garage next to the balcony out over his front lawn. He has a great water view from his balcony so the pool is a pretty special place, and he has also made much better use of his backyard, not only for himself and his kids but also for anybody who may choose to live in his home in the future. It is thinking differently that will separate you from the pack in a personal as well as professional capacity.

Think about the many instances where people have slayed the sacred cow and used the type of thinking that the Spin Cycle promotes. At some point in time, individuals have asked questions such as, 'What if a computer did not have to sit on your desk? What if you could take it with you?' Or, 'What if you did not have a hard roof on a car? What if you could remove it?' Someone after that asked, 'What if you did not have to remove the roof manually? What if you could do it automatically?' Somebody also asked the question, 'What if Listerine did not come in a bottle? What if you could take it with you?' This resulted in the revolutionary concept of the Listerine strip. Individuals around the world are asking themselves these types of breakthrough questions every day, and they are no different to you or me, it's just having the process, the courage and the understanding that nothing is sacred, and that nothing is beyond challenge.

Use the Spin Cycle to find and challenge the sacred cows in your world!

Key 12: Spider Web

A philosophy of mine has always been to look for constant and never-ending improvement in everything that I do. With this in mind, I created something called the Spider Web as a creative tool in 2003 (an improved and more efficient version of mind-mapping for those who have heard of mind-mapping). Essentially the Spider Web enables the user to quickly generate lots of different associations and non-associations for the topic they are brainstorming. The fun and user-friendly attributes of the Spider Web have seen this creative tool widely used not only in Australia but also in the United Kingdom and elsewhere to generate lots of ideas for people who need ideas in a hurry.

In the example shown in the colour section in the middle of the book, I have outlined a step-by-step development of a Spider Web to give you an idea of how you would use the Spider Web, using the example of a fictitious coffee shop searching for ideas as to how to stimulate sales in their small business.

The first step is to place a key word at the centre of the Spider Web, which reflects the topic that you wish to generate ideas for, and this word becomes the central focus of the discussion, so in this case I placed 'coffee' in the centre of the Spider Web. When thinking about that word, I want to know what other words come to mind by association. Write down these words on the page in the gaps that surround the key word. So for our coffee shop example, I have placed all the words that come to mind when I think of coffee — cup, sugar, books, cookies, smell and beans — in the first line of the web surrounding the word 'coffee'.

Once you have generated your first 'web' or line of words, take each of those individual words and use them to generate more related or unrelated words. The same process should then be repeated until the entire web is filled with words that are either related or unrelated to the topic you are looking for ideas for. Ask yourself when you think of this new word, what other words come to mind? This is step 2.

The end result (step 3) is that the Spider Web will give you dozens of words that will be both related or unrelated to the topic that you are brainstorming. For our coffee example, you can see that when I thought of cup, saucer came to mind, when I thought of saucer, I thought of spoon, spoon made me think of eggs, eggs made me think of chickens, chickens made me think of run, and running made me think of Nike, and so on.

Once you have all these associated or non-associated words written down in front of you, you simply select an individual word and start discussing what ideas come to you from that word, with regards to the topic you are brainstorming. Creative sessions are all about giving yourself stimuli from which to hook your ideas, and the words which you have written down on the Spider Web in effect become your stimulus for lateral thinking around a key focus. So for our coffee example I have looked at the completed web and selected an individual word at random (in this case I have circled ice cream), and I want to explore any ideas that come to mind when I think of ice cream and coffee (our key focus).

When I think about ice cream and coffee, an idea that comes to mind is perhaps to give away free ice creams to kids or pensioners when they buy a coffee. Perhaps we could develop a special coffee-flavoured ice cream to sell, or another idea could be that we sell an ice cream coffee, which involves adding a scoop of your favourite ice cream to your latte.

Next I circled 'trophy' on the web. Now, what does trophy make me think of? Maybe we could enter the coffee shop's special coffee roast into competitions to win a trophy for our coffee. Perhaps we could buy an award-winning coffee and sell it in our store, or we could potentially sponsor a school award for teachers and put the details of the competition into their coffee room. As you can see on the web shown here, I've followed the same pattern for the words 'grind' and 'spoon', using the words 'caught up' in the web to see what ideas I can think of when I think of coffee. You could also have unrelated words like 'police' in your web, which is great. Sometimes the words that are the most unrelated to your topic will give you the best ideas, so don't be afraid to use these words. Quite often in groups what seems like a silly association to start with ends up being a great gem of an idea. For example, when you think about police, perhaps you could run a special raffle from your store to raise money for the local police citizens youth club. Maybe you could allow the kids from the local police citizens youth club to bring a friend to the cafe and the friend receives a free coffee or soft drink.

As you can see, the Spider Web is a very simple and easy-to-use tool that can help you generate great ideas from a lateral and non-lateral point of view for your small business, your local charity, your kid's birthday party, or your multi-million-dollar organisation. One thing to remember when you use the Spider Web is speed. Do not edit your words as they come to you, write down the first thing that comes to mind; let the words flow and get them all down. Say you are working on ideas for car magazines, and you end up with a word like poodle in the web — you must still write it down because you never know, out of that word poodle you may get some of your best ideas! Also, it is important to remember that you can use the Spider Web either individually, as I have done with the coffee shop example, or just as successfully in a group. When using the Spider Web in group workshops, I usually have it printed out onto large flipchart-sized sheets to allow for increased ease of use.

The Spider Web, complete with instructions, is available from Blue Moon Creative. Please visit www.bluemooncreative.com.au.

Key 13: BiGNOA™

A system to generate new ideas, opportunities and actions for your business and life.

BiGNOA is essentially a process-driven five-step system that enables companies to effectively scrutinise their operations in order to identify their greatest future opportunities, and then design a structured action plan in order to secure those opportunities. It is a further development of the traditional and well-proven SWOT (strengths, weaknesses, opportunities, and threats) analysis that you may or may not have come across previously. The BiGNOA process is especially powerful when considering strategic issues at a business-unit or corporate level, although it can also be applied very successfully on a more personal level such as when considering a job or career change. It has been a very successful tool for me and the companies I have been using it with for the past few years, and I am delighted to be able to share it with you here.

My search for an alternative to the SWOT analysis began after many years of using SWOT as an analysis tool in my workshops. I found that the SWOT analysis tended to identify strengths and weaknesses from within the company or business, while the opportunities and threats tended to be identified as external to the company, simply through the way in which the process was structured. I also found that the individual running the SWOT analysis (often a manager or employee of the company) was often unable to step away sufficiently from their job role to honestly spot anything wrong with their company, while others were not able see anything right with their company or themselves when undertaking this process. Finally, I found that SWOT failed to capitalise on the opportunities presented by the analysis and did not commit anyone within the organisation to an action plan to fully realise the potential of its outcomes. So, unable to find an alternative process that addressed these issues, I came to develop my own system and I have called it BiGNOA.

The BiGNOA system allows you to identify the strengths and weaknesses of a company while also highlighting the many opportunities that may exist. It is set in a framework that allows the participants in a session to look for a positive future while still addressing any issues that may not be right currently. Perhaps, however, the greatest advantage that you will find with BiGNOA as opposed to the traditional SWOT is that the BiGNOA system gives you the opportunity to not only identify the most important or critical opportunities, but as importantly allows you to set in place an action plan and allocate roles to individuals to take advantage of these opportunities.

The process: what BiGNOA stands for and how it works
Before we get started, I would like to suggest that if you are planning to use the BiGNOA system with a group it is really beneficial to get an easel with flipchart paper, together with some bright, colourful pens for the group to use, and I would also suggest that you might want to grab some blu-tack or adhesive tape so that you can put the pages up on the walls around the room as you go.

BiGNOA stands for the following:

■ **Background information** — What background information do we need to consider, including threats, competitors, environment?

- **Great** — What's great about our company or the issue?

- **Nearlies** — What's not great yet? What's nearly right, and with work could be better or even great?

- **Opportunities** — What opportunities exist for us to take advantage of from the greats and not greats? Make a big list, then narrow to the critical three to five ideas.

- **Action plan** — What are the next steps to be taken to be able to capitalise on our opportunities? Who's doing what, and by when?

Step 1: Background information

This is an information-gathering exercise used to familiarise yourself with the issue/company/product under discussion and its position in the marketplace. It also brings everyone in the creative session up to speed with any issues and pertinent points that are relevant to the discussion. This part of the process should take no more than five or ten minutes, and should address areas such as market activity, competitor information, research, threats, an explanation of why the discussion is taking place and what you hope to achieve in the session.

Step 2: What's great?

Here the group should be identifying all the things that are great about the company, product or issue. What are the strengths, the things you are doing well, and the successes you / the company / the issue may be enjoying?

Pat yourselves on the back. What are you really good at, and what's going well? Make a big list of strengths and place these strengths on flipchart paper around the walls of the room. Use lots of colour and make sure that the writing on the page is legible.

Step 3: Nearlies

What's nearly right, but not quite there yet? Here we are looking to list all the things that aren't perfect yet about the company, product or issue, the things that could use some improvement. This part of the process is structured to allow you to look at the things that are 'nearly' great from a positive perspective, rather than looking at weaknesses which can be quite negative — although something is not great as yet, the premise is that we can make it great, leading towards a more positive outcome.

Step 4: Opportunities

The next step in BiGNOA is to generate a list of opportunities. When looking to build this list, either as a group or individually, you can review your previous two lists (the nearlies and the greats) to address all of the opportunities that exist — if things are nearly right, then the opportunity is to make them great. If things are currently great, ask yourself if there is an opportunity to make them even better.

The group should list any opportunities that it believes exist that will take the company or product forward. List anything that comes to mind as we are after a big list here. Use the pages on the walls around you as stimulants to build a long list of ideas. Some of the opportunities you think of may have nothing to do with those points of the previous two lists, and that's fine; put them on the opportunity list anyway.

Now that we have generated a list of opportunities, we can narrow down the list to the most important or critical opportunities. Which ideas from the list, if taken forward at this point, would be most beneficial to the company? Which ideas must be actioned? Narrow the list down to the top three to five ideas (the number is up to you or the group). One way of doing this is to give each person in the group three or four votes each, to indicate which ideas they think are the most important to take forward. Give each person a coloured pen and ask him or her to tick or mark the opportunities they feel are most important on the flipchart paper. There may be sixty ideas listed on the opportunities page. With their four votes, each person can vote for as many ideas as they see fit; they can put four marks on one idea if they believe that this is the most critical opportunity out of the whole list, or they can do two for one and two for another, or a single mark on each of four ideas, and so on. They are the individual's votes and no-one else's. As a guide, I generally allocate one vote for each fifteen opportunities; for example, if you have a group with seventy-five opportunities on the board, you might give each of the participants five votes each. Once each person has voted, circle the ideas that have the most votes. These are then the most critical opportunities to seize, as voted by the group (you will now perhaps have a list of three or more critical opportunities). Remember that at this point we are just looking for opportunities and not solutions to the opportunities — the solutions come in the next step of the process.

Step 5: The action plan

The action plan outlines what needs to be done in order to take the opportunities listed above forward to a point where it is possible to capitalise on the ideas — a very crucial step. It involves making decisions as to what needs to be done for each idea, who will be undertaking each task and by when, and committing it to paper. If the action plan is not outlined at this stage of the process then the ideas can potentially sit in a folder or on a piece of flipchart paper and never again see the light of day. Action plans without any allocation as to who is doing what and by when are just dreams without deadlines!

Remember that although we seized only three to five ideas to take forward to the next step, it does not mean that we cannot use any of the other opportunities that were generated. Just have them typed up and filed for next time, or perhaps you can even refer back to these opportunities once you have actioned the first three to five critical ideas.

BiGNOA really is a quick and efficient system that works to generate many ideas for the user whilst maintaining a positive framework. The most beneficial outcome of this process, apart from the fact that you can generate lots of quality ideas, is that the ideas are actioned and allocated. Another important advantage is that everyone from the group is given the opportunity to contribute to the process, so it will get buy-in from the entire group. Everyone has the option of contributing to each list, and they are also required to vote for the opportunities that they see as most critical. This means that even quiet shy individuals have the opportunity to contribute their ideas without feeling awkward, and it can help eliminate the possibility of one person dominating the discussions and forcing their ideas onto the rest of the group.

I have used the BiGNOA process with organisations of all shapes and sizes, both in Australia and overseas. From movie companies to sports drinks companies to telecommunications companies to magazines to hotel chains, the process has proven to be equally successful. The process has many varied applications, and I have found it can even be effective when writing business plans or when doing company and personal planning and evaluations. BiGNOA is now being used in many parts of the world, including the USA, the UK and even Israel. It's a simple process that is easy to implement and explain, and that in itself is a key to successful idea generation and its execution.

Key 14: How do you judge a good idea anyway?

This is a very good question, and one that has been asked of me many times. It is also a question that plagues many people such as Jane, a human resources manager. During a lunch break in one of my sessions, Jane approached me wanting to know how to judge her ideas. 'I am an ideas person ... I have hundreds of ideas,' she said. 'I drive the girls in the office nuts with the amount of ideas I have, but I always get stuck when I start to think about whether they will work or not … what do I do?'

The most important thing to do initially is to get everything down on paper. Don't judge your ideas before you even start — write them down. If you tend to come up with ideas on a regular basis, you might even want to consider a book for your ideas, somewhere that you can gather all of your ideas and they won't get lost. I use a book to collect interesting names for companies, projects, promotions and products. I also jot down sayings, quotes, concepts and great lines from movies, as you never know when you might need a little inspiration. So many people keep their ideas on bits of scrap paper, on old spiral pads, or on the back of napkins. It's great that they are getting committed to paper, but it's also very easy to lose them. Transcribe these valuable ideas as quickly as possible from odd scraps of paper into a book set aside for just this purpose; that way you know where they are when you need them.

The importance of writing your valuable ideas down on paper was brought home to me when I was running a workshop for a major soft drink company in Sydney. We had spent much of the day designing ideas for the company's South Pacific Region sales promotion. The session had been going very well and everyone had been contributing ideas and coming up with some really exciting concepts. The good news was that they were responding to the stimulants that I was throwing at them and letting themselves go, but throughout the entire process the manager of the team, and the organiser of the day, kept impatiently asking me, 'When do we get to pick out the best ideas? When do we get to look at the reality of the ideas? You know, pick out the good ones, because some of these ideas won't work or won't fit our budget.' He was most perturbed that we were not getting down to the judging of the ideas as we went along. I asked him to bear with me and just go with the flow, but I could see that this was really testing him. In this day and age people are encouraged to judge ideas instantly on the spot. We are brought up in a world of rights and wrongs, and are constantly told 'that won't work because …', or, 'what a silly idea'. Consequently, a great deal of the time our ideas are judged before we even get them down on paper or say them out aloud. In this way, very valuable ideas can be missed and never see the light of day. Often those ideas, although not totally developed, could be the start of something great. So get those ideas down on paper and then worry about how to use them!

Once your ideas are actually down on paper, you can then think about what criteria you may want the ideas to meet. Do you remember the fourth and fifth steps of the Creative Dancea brainstorming model, the C and the E? The C is for Criteria, and the E is for Evaluating your ideas. These two steps are useful not only when doing a brainstorm but also when you are evaluating your own ideas. Take the time to sit down and think about what criteria your new ideas would have to meet in order to be successful. Write them all down, select the top three to five, and then set about evaluating your ideas against your most important criteria. You might even decide to construct a success grid as described in the Creative Dancea process, in order to clearly identify which idea works best for your selected outcomes. In this way you can make the most of your ideas — you can collect them, articulate them and then run them through a process in order to select the ideas which have the most chance of success against your chosen criteria — it's that easy.

I floated this concept to Jane, the HR person at the lunch, and she was very excited. Finally she had a way of judging her ideas rather than using guesswork! Jane called over the other girls from the office to explain the process, and you could almost see the relief on their faces as it had become tiresome for them to hear Jane constantly dropping new ideas and concepts onto the table without knowing what to do with them. So you see it can be very frustrating both for an ideas person and for those that they share their ideas with if there isn't any process by which to judge an idea.

Another way to judge your ideas is to research the concept. Now this does not necessarily mean having to spend a lot of money with research companies, particularly if you own a small business. What I am talking about is undertaking your own research.

The first step is to write down and clearly articulate your idea. Ask yourself questions such as:

- What is the concept?

- Who is it targeted at; that is, who would be the people who would benefit most by using the idea?

- What will be the benefit of the idea to them; that is, how should they use the idea?

■ Why is it different to what you have done before, or why is it different to anything else that might be available?

■ How will you tell people about it?

■ How will people get to use it or do it?

Once you have the answers to these questions and other questions that you yourself may have come up with, you then need to go about finding people who fit the target audience and run the idea by them to gauge their reaction. Depending on how sensitive the idea is, you may need to be careful who you share the concept with, but it is another great way to test your ideas. Once you have it clear in your mind what the concept is about, who it suits, why it is different and why people should buy it, then you need to go and ask the people that you expect to buy it whether they think the idea is sound. If you are introducing a new product or service to the market and you are a member of a community club, sports club or parents committee (and providing the people you are talking to are roughly in your target market for the idea) then there is your research group. If it's an idea for the office then gather a few people from the office and run your idea by them.

Here are a couple of things to look out for in your research group. Try to select those folks who are open-minded, who are generally open to new ideas, who are constructive and moving forwards themselves, with a positive and encouraging although realistic view of the future. Be wary of the energy suckers who hate anything new and are definitely opposed to change, as they will just endeavour to suck the life out of you and your idea. If you do happen to run your idea past someone like this, accept their point of view but remember they are not the only point of view (although some will have you think otherwise). Encourage these people to be honest in their opinions about your idea — both the good and the not so good. Always ask for both sides. This is another situation where you can use the PPC approach that is discussed in chapter 2.

Ultimately though, no matter which process you may use to judge an idea and what results your research may show, you still need the courage to fly with an idea. The suggestions above can take some of the guesswork out of the process but at the end of the day there's no guarantee that your idea will work. Perhaps a better question to ask yourself at this point is whether you have the courage to get behind your idea and take it out to the world. This failure of courage more than anything is what can keep a great idea from ever seeing the light of day!

While working in the radio industry I came across a man by the name of Barry Chapman, who was the CEO of one of the Australian radio networks at that time. Although we did not see eye to eye in every instance (and that can be healthy), I did learn a valuable lesson from him that I still carry with me to this day. Barry was unquestionably an ideas man. If he had an idea he thought it through, devised a strategy, gathered the resources required and then he would just run with it. He had enormous conviction in his ideas, and although some ideas worked and others didn't, he lived up to his motto: 'I'll never die wondering!' That lesson has stayed with me to this day, and I wish more people could be like him. Don't let perfection or fear stand in the way of your good ideas!

THE FIVE TRAITS OF THE CREATIVE THINKER

4

When you think of the people who inspire you creatively, would you say that they tend to have certain characteristics in common? Think of your heroes, whether they are people within your family, artists, friends, sports people, famous leaders, spokespeople for human rights, or maybe a poet or an author. You might perhaps have listed people such as Walt Disney, Einstein, Bill Gates, Mother Teresa, Mandela, Lady Diana or Steven Spielberg. Maybe it is your mum, your first-grade teacher or your best friend. Often you will find that these people do indeed have certain traits in common.

I have listed below the most common five traits that I have discovered creative people possess. This sums up the characteristics that I believe are to be encouraged and fostered, both within yourself and in others around you, in order to make this world a more interesting, unique and creative place. Practise these five traits and unlock your creative talents.

1. Confidence

We discussed the importance of having belief in your own creative ability earlier in the book. Creative individuals tend to have an inner confidence, such that when faced with a problem, opportunity or challenge, they know they will always find a solution. They know it may not always be the best solution and that it may take some time, but they do have an unquestionable inner confidence in their own ability. Some say it openly, some just get on with it in silence until they have a solution, but either way they know an idea will come to them.

It is always great when we have this sort of confident thinker in the room during workshops. When I give the room a puzzle or brainteaser, these people always ask lots of questions, ensure they have all the information, then go quiet whilst they go to work thinking about the solution until they reach an outcome. In contrast, others in the room spend sixty seconds thinking about it, and if they can't get it in that time, roll their eyes back and say, 'Oh this is too hard, I never get these things.' Well, little wonder! These people are programming themselves not to find solutions, while those with confidence just proceed at their own pace and work their way through the puzzle, always moving towards finding a solution.

The good news is that you can develop your own confidence by having faith in your ability and approaching your problems or opportunities with the firm belief that you will come up with an answer. Many people need to actively boost their confidence levels, whether they are performers, sportspeople, politicians, media presenters or simply office workers who want to develop their inner strength. It starts by saying to yourself, either inside your head or out loud to yourself or others, 'I can get this,' or, 'I can do this.' It may sound silly, but if you do it regularly you might surprise yourself — it does work. When placed in a tricky situation, or when you need to find a way to do something, you should say to yourself, under your breath, 'I can do this, come on, I can do this.' It is a bit like a subtle version of what Australian tennis ace Lleyton Hewitt does when he yells out, 'Come on!', only you can do it in a whisper under your breath so no-one else hears. Either way, it works! The brain can't distinguish between what is imaginary and what is real, and when you program yourself this way, your brain will search for the evidence to prove you right. As they say, 'Say it and believe it!'

People with confidence are also comfortable with the prospect of making a few mistakes. When you see a young child learning to walk, do they stand up first go? No. They get up, and down they go again, and so it goes for some time until they get it. We must learn that not every idea is going to be a good one and not every idea will work, and we must also learn to have the confidence to wobble, just like a young child learning to walk. So have the confidence to speak up and have the faith to execute with passion, knowing that you're going to make a few mistakes but also knowing that your mistakes will be learning experiences and they will make you better, stronger, wiser and more creative. As the saying goes, to make no mistakes, do nothing, say nothing and be nothing! Think about all of the great achievers in business, sport, charities, politics or any human endeavour; all the great achievers have made more than their fair share of mistakes. If you spoke with them, I suspect they would say that their mistakes were one of the things that made them great. As country singer Dolly Parton once said, 'The way I see it, if you want a rainbow, you have to put up with the rain.'

2. Curiosity

Creative types all tend to be curious. They want to know what else can be done, how can it be done differently, what is next, why can't we do it that way, or even who says? Curious people really are creative people, the ones asking questions that lead to new ways of doing things. They want to open up new frontiers and make things better.

Freethinkers and creative types ask questions both of themselves and others. They are always wondering about things, asking questions such as, 'What would happen if … ?' They are often unhappy with the status quo, and some might say they get a bit bored when they are not being challenged. That does not mean that you must act on every idea or that you must change things just for the sake of change, but you should always ask the questions.

In a business sense, creative people are always looking at their businesses to see what they can improve or make more efficient. They tend to attack themselves first before their opposition has a chance to, with the view that, 'If it ain't broke, break it!' Again, this doesn't mean that you must implement everything that you come up with, and it is not change for the sake of change, it is the process of challenging yourself and asking the questions of yourself and the business that is important.

In a personal sense, creative thinkers are always looking for the next interesting thing to do, perhaps going on a holiday to a new destination, buying an unusual present for a friend, finding a unique book to read, or simply making a different recipe for dinner. These people are happy to experiment and won't be deterred by failure, so if something does not work at first they will think of other ways to possibly make it work and go from there.

You may recall a scene from *Dead Poets Society*, staring Robin Williams, in which Williams is a poetry teacher in an American boys college. In this particular scene, the teacher has the boys in his class stepping up onto the teacher's desk at the front of the study hall. He encourages them to stand there for a moment and look around, and then he says, 'Boys, strive to find your own voice; just when you think you know something, you must try to find another way to do it.' What a wonderful movie for anyone wanting to discover his or her own potential.

The curious mind of the creative thinker is fuelled by questions, and I do believe strongly that one of the greatest traits that you can develop to be more creative is to be curious about everything you do (and the easiest way to do that is to ask lots of questions of yourself and others). All great discoveries and breakthroughs come as a result of questions asked by a curious mind. Why shouldn't the next breakthrough come from your curious mind fuelled by one of your questions? Einstein would ask questions even when he knew the answer! He is quoted as saying, 'I have no special gift — I am only passionately curious.' Fuel your curiosity by always looking for options, asking questions and challenging things in your mind.

3. Persistence

No matter who your creative hero is, you will probably find that they are determined, very focused, rarely defeated and unusually persistent. I believe that persistence is one of the most important ingredients that a true creative thinker can possess, because it takes persistence to continually ask questions in order to find alternate and better ways to do things.

For the majority of people, if they cannot find a solution to a puzzle or brainteaser within the first sixty seconds they think it is all too hard, and you begin to hear comments such as, 'This is too hard, I am so stupid, I'm not creative and I can't get it.' Little wonder they don't get it, as they won't persist with trying to find the answer beyond the first minute. It takes persistence to push beyond the known to find another way to do something, and it takes persistence to continually ask more and better questions to get to the solution to a problem. When it becomes hard the quitters leave it to the freethinkers because they know they will not quit, that the creative thinkers will persist because they know that their has to be another answer, and they are going to find it. Never give up; there is always another way, and the person who does not quit is quite often the person who discovers the new ideas and breaks through to the new frontiers. Albert Einstein was known to have said, 'It's not that I am smart, it's just that I stay with the problem longer.' Do you hang in there and ponder issues, problems and options, or do you give up?

A good friend of mine works in public relations, and she says that when she is looking for an idea for a client she sits around until an idea comes to her. It may take a while, and it may take many cups of coffee, but she sits there until the idea comes because in the end she knows that it will come! Now that is persistence. These are the type of people that I enjoy working with, people who do not give up when the thinking process gets hard; those who persevere until they are satisfied with the outcome. This friend of mine is very successful at what she does, and with persistence like that, you begin to see why. Is this not the sort of person you would like to have working on your business?

Put another way, questions are the things that prime your creative pump up there in your imagination. Once the pump is primed, you still sometimes need to have the persistence to pump like mad to start the ideas flowing, otherwise nothing will come of it. It is true that occasionally the answers will just come to you when you least expect it and they flow very easily, but on other occasions you have to be prepared to work hard to find great ideas. The funny thing is that most of the really great ideas are often the ones that come at the back end of your thinking session. Once you have found the easy and obvious answers, you start to prime the pump for the 'what else could we do' ideas, and it is usually these ideas that have real value, and these ideas will only come with true persistence. Indeed, the first part of the session is like picking off the low-hanging fruits (the obvious ideas). The real pick of the crop usually comes from the last third of the ideas conceived in the session; getting out there on a limb to grab the best fruit takes real persistence.

4. Courage

It has been written that great leaders need courage, and that is very true. To bring great ideas to life, the creative thinker needs a certain amount of courage. The question is, are you willing to make use of it? The creative thinker is willing to give their ideas a go, throw caution to the wind and take a chance. In saying that, courage does not mean implementing your ideas in a reckless manner — you must think through your ideas thoroughly, plan effectively for all outcomes, build in contingency plans if need be, develop the action plan, and then go for it. It just means having the confidence to believe in your ideas, and in the cases where you have thought it through, making them happen.

The sad thing is that in boardrooms in different parts of the world as you read this page, there are good ideas generated that will never see the light of day. Why is that? Because somebody had an idea that they whispered to themselves at the back of their mind, but they didn't have the courage to speak up. This is one of the driving forces behind me writing this book, to encourage people to believe in themselves, believe in their ideas and have the courage to be heard. Ordinary people have great ideas every day: why can't that person be you or me? Have the courage to speak up and have your ideas heard. The worst thing that can happen is for someone to not like your idea, in which case you can think of another one. You have an infinite number of ideas within you, and undoubtedly some of them are great ideas — but you must speak up. Having the courage to speak up and have your ideas heard takes some getting used to. You need to develop a thick skin, and it all depends on how you approach it in your own mind. Thinking of the ideas is the easy bit; it is saying them out loud that can sometimes be the challenge.

Everybody has an idea in the shower. It is the person who dries off and does something with the idea who makes a difference. So towel off and let's go! Don't worry about other people. As Einstein said, great spirits will always encounter violent opposition from mediocre minds.

5. Time

Creative thinkers know the value of time, particularly the value of taking time out to think. They are not caught up in the habitual day-to-day routine of endless meetings, phone calls and emails, and they take time every so often to sit quietly and think about their world. Creative thinkers value their thinking time and they schedule it accordingly. Even if it is just a thirty-minute walk in the street or park at lunch, they take the time to contemplate a particular issue, or at other times they may just have a general wander to people-watch or to take the time to ask themselves a few questions.

When I worked in radio, we were constantly asked to generate ideas for clients. Many clients wanted an idea the very same day they gave us the brief, which of course was often possible to do, but if the client wanted a really great idea they needed to know that they should give us some time to think about it, to let it sit in our subconscious. Eventually clients realised that if they just wanted any idea pumped out by the station they could demand it the same day, but if they wanted something a bit special they had to give us some time.

Naturally, because of what I do I spend a lot of time talking to people about their creative processes. I was fortunate enough to once share an apartment in Sydney with a guy nicknamed Rusty, who was a creative director of the radio station I worked at. Because we were sharing an apartment and I knew him so well, I always felt as though I could ask him to do me favours and get scripts knocked up quickly when I needed to. But over time, I came to appreciate that Rusty did his best work when I gave him plenty of time to ponder a script. He was one of these people who needed to let his subconscious think through ideas and to expose himself to outside stimulants to be able to write a unique and special script. It was a valuable lesson that I took to heart — I still have Rusty write all of my radio scripts, but I know to give him a week to think about it, and he never lets me down.

I remember on one occasion he had even gone into work at 4 am as a great idea had come to him in the wee hours, and he just had to get it down. Most creatives will tell you the same thing: 'Let me think about it.' You are no different. Give yourself time to think, and — along with all your other projects for the day — budget time into your day just to think. Call it 'you' time. Time has to become one of things you value; true freethinkers value every minute of the day and take time out to think.

Also remember that your thinking time can be used for more than just generating specific solutions for issues or promotional ideas — use the time to come up with unique methods of implementing those ideas. You have allocated time to explore potential ideas, so why not take it to the next level and make the implementation as unique as the concept. I once facilitated a thinking session for a sales promotions company that was in a competitive pitch situation with regards to new and exciting promotional ideas for a soup company client of theirs. We were outdoors in a national park near Sydney Harbour (a great spot to create). We had used the Creative Dancea process, and had generated hundreds of new ideas and narrowed it down to the best three or four for them to test on their soup client. The group were ready to move on to the next issue on their agenda when I suggested that there might be some other angles that they may want to consider regarding this client, since they were in a competitive pitch for the business.

I explained to the group that the thinking session perhaps should not be limited just to the promotional idea; that is, it could be extended to the presentation itself.

I urged them to consider where they would present, who would present, how they would get the client there, what food they should serve, should they play music, what's the leave-behind document going to look like, and so on. So often we think about creativity as being all about the big idea, but in reality it can extend way beyond this, and we must remember that there are new or different ways to do just about anything as long as we take the time to think about it.

So, back to the promotional ideas for our soup client. It just so happened that the promotions were designed to be based around football, so I had the team work on coming up with unique ways to answer the above questions so that they related back to football, and the result was that the team decided to present the proposal to their client in a football locker room at one of the main football stadiums. They all dressed in football jerseys, and even went to the trouble of finding out the client's favourite team and having that team's jersey there on the day for the client to wear. There were footy tunes playing through a stereo when the client arrived, and they even had a half-time break in the presentation for some Gatorade refreshment, and so it went. Their unique presentation backed up a great idea, and as a result they won the business, which was worth nearly AUD$1 million dollars. It all shows that quite often there are many aspects that we take for granted, but a little freethinking and time can make the difference between mediocre and outstanding!

Remember also that the principles that we apply to our business lives also work just as well in our home lives. If you are perhaps cooking a special meal for the family, think about the little extras that could make the evening that little bit more special — candles, the right music, perhaps a hand-written menu, invitations for the family members to attend, silly presents or perhaps a unique location for the dinner, in the garage or a bedroom. Who knows what ideas you may come up with; just don't limit yourself to thinking that you have to have the *BIG* idea to be creative. You can apply your creative talents in so many little areas that quite often add up to being a great overall idea. You are faced with little problems all day long, and every one is a great opportunity for you to apply your freethinking mind to other possibilities. It is a matter of thinking through the problem, breaking it down, and then taking the time to allow your conscious and unconscious minds to think through it and ponder it.

It's funny hearing corporate managers and executives say that they can't afford the time to be out of the office thinking. My reply is to ask them what one good idea is worth to their business. Imagine if a CEO had one great idea that was able to generate revenue each week for the next ten years; what could that be worth to the business? When people say they can't afford the time, I would prefer they ask themselves if they can afford *not* to take the time.

Leonardo da Vinci once said, 'The greatest geniuses sometimes achieve more when they work less.' Think about that!

5 CHILDREN

From a very early age our belief in our innate creativity and capacity for generating ideas and the quality of those ideas has been moulded by those around us — from parents to teachers, coaches and even friends and society — to make us the people we are today. It is vital for us to recognise the importance and vibrancy of children, and to encourage and foster creative and original thinking in our children as they grow so that we give them every opportunity to be the very best that they can be.

I was never short on imagination or on ideas about how to make a dollar! When I was five years old my family was living in Central Queensland in a township called Biloela. My father worked for a bank, and being a relatively young bank manager he was required to entertain clients in order to impress them and attract their business. One night dad had several of his important clients over for dinner, and as a treat for the clients' children my mum had made meringues for dessert, one of my favourites. After the main meal, mum handed me a large tin of freshly made meringues and asked me to hand them out to the children at the party. I disappeared out to the backyard of our house to distribute the meringues to the other children as requested. About five minutes later, one of the kids went into the living room where the adults were chatting and having drinks, and asked his dad for five cents. When his father quizzed the child on why he wanted five cents, he said, 'I want to buy some meringues.' I figured my mum's meringues were the best, and hence were worth every bit of the five cents I had decided to charge the other kids for them! I have reprinted mum's recipe at the back of the book, and you never know, you might be able to sell some yourself … just use your imagination![12]

Encouraging
CHILDREN TO BE CREATIVE

I believe that it is important to reflect back to our childhood from time to time to remember that special period of our lives, when there were no barriers, no rules, and every day was full of challenges, questions, exploration and new learning. Although I recognise that education and the process of growing up requires a certain degree of conformity to society's dictates, we must also remember to nurture and feed the little creative minds that are

---

12   Appendix D: Mum's meringue recipe.

growing within our children, rather than ignore them or punish their behaviour because it makes our lives temporarily easier or it is outside the norm. Remember that questions are the cornerstones of our learning and our creativity — don't curb that precious quality!

Have you ever seen parents telling their children to 'shut up', 'stop asking questions', 'don't do this, don't do that', or school teachers who tell children that clouds can't be green, or to stop daydreaming? How about those teachers who seem to gain great pleasure from telling children what they get wrong, as opposed to what they get right — goodness knows I had some of these teachers at school. I recognise that it is often easier said than done, but we must try to encourage as much as we possibly can.

A former colleague phoned me one day and we ended up having an interesting discussion about children's thinking processes. Elizabeth has two children and was herself a corporate presenter. She was telling me the story of the time that she entered a room at home to find her little girl having a wonderful time playing in the fish food, which was carefully spread across their timber floor, under the fish tank. It was everywhere! Her daughter had emptied the entire contents of a packet of fish food flakes onto the floor, and was enthralled with the designs she was able to make as she ran her hands through the piles of food. When Elizabeth entered the room, her immediate reaction was to say, 'What is going on here young lady?' But before Elizabeth could get the words out, her daughter said, 'Look at all the pretty pictures mummy.' This threw Elizabeth for a moment

— what pictures? Once Elizabeth took the time to sit down with her daughter, she was captivated by what this little bubble of imagination could see in the fish food spread throughout the room. 'Look mummy, here is an elephant, here's a house, and here is a puppy dog,' she said as she proudly displayed her masterpieces. The lesson that Elizabeth learnt that day was to never assume that her children were being intentionally destructive or naughty when they made a mess.

Don't automatically assume the worst, as most of the time their actions are not calculated, they are just exploring their imagination and being creative. There is often logic to their thinking and what they are doing that may not be immediately obvious to us adults. Maybe they are simply creating and feeding their own seed of imagination … it's at this age that we need to feed, nurture and fan these freethinking young minds. When was the last time you sat on the floor and played with a toy, rolled in the grass or splashed in a drain whilst the rain poured down?

One of the most gratifying things about being a presenter is the opportunity to meet so many new people and hear and share their stories. I remember meeting a guy in a workshop in Melbourne recently who spoke to me about creativity and his son. We were talking about the types of stimulation that can assist in getting people to think differently about their personal and work lives. He told me a story about his son and the time they share together every night before his son goes to bed. Each night the two of them head off to the bedroom and, as part of his son's good-night ritual, he reads his son a story. They had been doing this for some time when his son started to ask questions about the book and the next piece to come in the story. His dad then started to close the book and make up his own storylines in response to his son's questions, which was initially a bit challenging as this was way out of the normal bounds of his creative thinking as a leader of a multi-national organisation. He was used to strategies, bullet points, presentations and board meetings, and wasn't used to using his imagination and creativity in this sort of way. In fact, it had probably been forty-five years since he sat down with crayons and markers or imagined the world of gremlins, leprechauns and fairies at the bottom of the garden.

Anyway, as the weeks progressed the stories became more and more elaborate, and he started to get more and more interested in the prospect of the next story instalment at his son's bedtime. In fact, when this CEO and dad was talking to me his face lit up as he told the story about how he was using his imagination and creativity to come up with wonderful stories and mysteries regarding his own fictitious characters. He said it really was something that he never had dreamed of doing, but the more he did it the more he found he enjoyed it. He also felt it was having a big impact on his business, as he found himself more and more comfortable about thinking differently and using a kind of thinking to imagine outcomes for his business. The other gratifying thing that he made comment about was that gradually his son was taking over the storytelling from him, which was encouraging his son to use his imagination and intellect to construct new chapters in their own storytelling.

I really think that this is a fantastic story, and I would encourage anyone to nurture the imagination of their children to allow them to create elaborate stories in the world of fantasy and imagination. It is something that many corporates do not have the opportunity or make the time to do.

One exercise that I do quite often at the start of my workshops is to partner people up with someone that they may not know particularly well and have them write a fictitious story about them. I have them write the story for three minutes, and — to encourage a flow of ideas — their pen must not leave the page. The idea behind this task is that the attendees of the workshop get to sit for three or four minutes and completely use their imagination. The only thing that is true about the story they are writing about the partner is their name. Once they have said, 'I would like to introduce my new friend …', then from that point forward the story is completely fictitious. I also encourage them to write bizarre fantasy stories — in fact the more bizarre the better! It is quite amazing to see people's faces as they write their elaborate stories, and I always love seeing the snickers as they think about the funny things they are writing. Without a doubt, somebody always walks up to say how much they enjoyed this exercise because it is the first time in many, many years they have had the chance to use their imagination in this way, and I encourage them to not lose that sense of imagination as we move forward to the more structured parts of the day. It also helps the attendees prove to themselves that their imagination does exist, it's just that we don't take the time or make the effort to leverage this part of our minds to create new ideas for our personal lives or our businesses very often, if at all!

So you might ask, how *do* you feed the creative minds of children? We must feed the creative minds of our children by encouraging them to ask questions, allowing them to daydream, giving them quiet time to draw *outside* the lines, to make the sky green, and to make a mess from time to time, all without getting in trouble. Ask them questions and let them use their own creative minds to come up with wonderful, imaginative ideas. Whether they are right or wrong doesn't matter, and it may take some time, but this encouragement to explore their own imagination is very important.

I was with another gentleman in a workshop in Adelaide and he relayed a story about how he too reads stories to his son in the evening. He recalled the time when in his story his son had a magic wand that he had received from a gremlin. With this magic wand his son had turned himself into a puppy. The father let this little boy tell a most wondrous story, until the boy realised that because he was now a puppy dog he was unable to use the wand to turn himself back into a little boy. Rather than the father jumping in to solve the problem, he let the little boy solve his own problem. Although it took a little time, the boy finally realised that he could carry the magic wand in his mouth back to the gremlin who had originally given it to him, and he allowed the gremlin to perform the magic required to once again transform the puppy dog back into a little boy. As the father relayed the story, his face grew brighter and brighter, with a broader and broader smile. This is the type of activity that you can perform with any child to allow them to use their imagination and step outside the norms into the world where rather than thinking about what is, they can explore the world of what could be.

We must take these little flickers of creativity in children and fan them to create a flame, and further foster these flames until they become raging fires, and further fuel these fires to become blazing wild-fires of creative ideas and imaginative thoughts. Some of the children who need their fires fanned are working in the office right next to you. They have just never had anyone to encourage or foster their creative ideas, and they too need a coach or teacher to bring out the best in their creative ability. Their flicker is there, they just need someone to hold the fan. We all need to have those people around us who will challenge us, stimulate us, encourage us, and most of all be a friend who will bring out the best in us.

I was working with a lawyer not long ago who had a few months earlier attended one of my creativity workshops. Thankfully she enjoyed the workshop, and then had me present to her law firm. At the end of the session, this particular lawyer rose to her feet to say thanks for my presentation (she liked it the second time around just as much as the first). During the thank you she relayed a story that following the first time she had seen me speak she went home determined to break out of her usual habits. Her husband was away on a business trip and so, as I had suggested to the group, I had challenged her to sleep on a different side of the bed. She did this, and when she woke up in the morning her four-year-old son was standing at the foot of the bed.

His first comment was to ask why she was sleeping on daddy's side of the bed. She replied, 'Because we had this man speak to us during the week and he said we should try new things, and I am sleeping on daddy's side of the bed to see what it is like and to try something different.' The little boy, being a typical four year old, replied, 'No mummy, you should sleep on your side of the bed, that's daddy's side of the bed.' The lawyer then spent some time talking with her son to assure him that it was okay to try new things, and that he too should always look to do things differently.

That evening when she went to her son's bedroom to tuck him into bed, she found the bed completely stripped and the pillow at the opposite end of the bed. The message from the little boy was that he too wanted to do things differently. Apparently he stayed at that end of the bed for four months, until he decided to change once again and to head back to the original end of the bed for his good night's sleep.

We should take these lessons and encourage children and those around us to realise their own creative ability. We must encourage not only ourselves, but also those we work with, live with, and share our lives with, to break out, try new things, and have the confidence to think differently. Our own self-talk must be positive and come from the belief that you are creative and that you have the qualities of a creative person. You were born with them and you had them at an early age; it is society that takes away a lot of your creativity. Now is the time to learn from the children around you, act your shoe size, and bring back the beauty of your childhood. I will leave this section with a great quote from a guy called Neil Postman, which says, 'Children enter schools as question marks and leave as periods.'

Don't take yourself or the world around you so seriously. Have a laugh, smile, and let the creative good times flow.

6 OTHER STUFF

I have put together a few bits and pieces that I have written over the years for newsletters and in-house publications that have proven to be really popular with clients and workshop groups alike. They didn't fit into any of the existing chapters of the book, but they are fun and I thought you might enjoy reading them. I hope they stimulate further thought or discussion on the topics involved!

HOW TO GET AWAY FROM THE EVERYDAY, EVERY DAY

I am sure everyone can relate to that wonderful feeling we experience when we have just returned from a holiday. We've had maybe two or three weeks away from the everyday, and we come home feeling a million dollars tanned, relaxed, focused, with not a care in the world.

Within a few days of being back at work, the roof caves in, and we're back to feeling exactly how we felt before we went away. This made me ask the question: why is that? And why can't we always feel like we do at the end of a holiday? Why is it that we need to have two or three weeks away from the everyday in order to feel human again?

With that in mind, here are a couple of strategies that I have picked up from workshops and implemented myself in order to escape the everyday, every day.

1. Start the weekend early

I was working with a guy from a credit union recently and he mentioned that every Friday he goes into work an hour or two early so that he can leave an hour or two earlier than normal. During summer, he hits the beach near his home at 4.30 or 5.00 o'clock in the afternoon. He spends a good hour to an hour-and-a-half on the beach, and in this way he starts his weekend early. He has a three-day weekend, as opposed to just the norm of Saturday and Sunday. It's a really interesting idea. Think about something you love doing, and get to it early on a Friday afternoon. Whether it's catching up with a friend for a drink, seeing a movie, going shopping or sitting in the park reading a book — when you do something fun on a Friday afternoon, it certainly makes you feel as though you've had an early start on the weekend.

2. Dedicate specific time
for reading on the weekend

Grab a freshly brewed coffee or pot of tea and some cookies; find a tree or a couch, some sun and a book. It's amazing how just having an hour or two on the couch indulging in a good book can make you feel like new. This 'me time' is essential not only for the relaxation benefits of chilling out, but also for the stimulation it gives your creative mind.

3. Get a good night's sleep
or have an afternoon nap

One thing that happens when we are on holiday is that we take the time to rest at any time of the day, and we also take the time to read a book. Why? Because we can. When we are on holidays, we don't feel guilty about having a snooze during the afternoon or taking the time to read a good book. Why should the normal week be any different? My suggestion is not only to get a good night's sleep a few nights a week — that is, be in bed at 8.30 or 9.00 o'clock — but also, on the weekend, to take a nap on a Saturday or Sunday afternoon if you feel like it. It does wonders for your body, your spirit and your clarity of thought.

4. Eat well

Yes, I know a lot has been written in magazines, books and newspapers about diet, but it's amazing how few people are listening. Eat well! This builds your immune system, increases your clarity of thought and boosts your spirit, and it also gives you more energy than you will know what to do with. I'm not talking about a diet; it's all about changing the way you eat. Cut back on carbohydrates, fat, sugar, alcohol, and junk food. This will give you lots more energy, and once again, you'll feel like you are on holidays. It is surprising how when we go on holidays, we change our diet and eat better, because we put the time in to either make nice food or find good food.

5. Meet new people

When we are on holidays and are relaxed, we seem to feel comfortable meeting and talking to new people. When in your normal routine, whether it is at a bar, on the beach or at a party, make a point of shaking hands with new people, and in doing so stimulate your spirit and your creative mind. Sometimes an interesting conversation when you are relaxed and learning something new can give you a different approach to your world and the world around you. You may have recently thought about taking up a new sport or hobby or changing your direction in life — talking to new people can bring these things to life and make them a reality. You'll be amazed at what opens up for you when you put your thoughts 'out there'.

6. Watch a movie

It is surprising how when we are on holidays, we don't feel guilty about taking time out — an afternoon or an evening — to go and watch a movie. Why wait for the weekend? Catch a flick during the week and help yourself feel like you are on holidays.

7. Find some new scenery

When we are on holidays, the new environment constantly stimulates our senses. Holidays break up our routine, and we are happily forced to experience a new schedule, new scenery, new activities, and different people. Why not play foreigner in your own town — take the long way home and explore the back streets of your neighbourhood or city. Or find out if you can catch a ferry or train to work once a week. How can you not feel like you are holidaying when you're cruising along the harbour as the sun is rising? Why not hop out of bed a bit earlier than usual and watch the sun come up from a good vantage point with an espresso? Go to a different place for lunch, order something you've never ordered before, or take your lunch to a different corner of the park near your office. Borrow some CDs from a friend or channel-flick on your radio at work for some new sounds. On the weekend, take a drive over a bridge and picnic at a place you've never been to before. Or jump on a train or ferry with your camera and go sight-seeing in your city. Your mind and spirit are constantly craving new sounds, sights, smells and experiences. Being in holiday mode could be as simple as going to a different beach or running on a different track to the one you tend to routinely navigate towards.

8. Get a babysitter

Those of you with young kids may have been reading points one to seven thinking that all of this is easy to do but what happens if you have kids? Plan ahead like you would with a holiday and book in an aunt, grandparent or friend for a mid-week night so you can catch that film you have wanted to see or go for a nice dinner. Or better still, get your babysitter to take the kids for the night so you can have that good night's sleep and a leisurely breakfast.

9. Do that 'thing I have always wanted to do' today!

When you're on holiday, you're more likely to try scuba diving, have a surf class, para-sail, climb a mountain, take an exotic cooking class or take up belly dancing. Why wait till you are on holidays in Australia or half way around the world to achieve one of these goals? Seize the day and take on one of the things you've always wanted to do. Sure, you may need to make a few calls, do some research and book ahead, but the internet or the *Yellow Pages* will easily help bring your sky dive or salsa class closer to reality, perhaps even this weekend!

So there you have it; a few pointers as to how you can make the most of every day to get away from the everyday! Why wait for holidays to feel relaxed, less stressed, clear headed, stimulated and focused? Start today by taking on one of these strategies! They work, they're easy, anyone can do them anywhere, and they bring great results. Now, take the afternoon off and enjoy your holiday!

Problems, problems, problems!

While conducting a workshop in Tokyo recently, I struck up a casual conversation with the CEO of the company I was working with. We were chatting about various aspects of creative thinking and the processes involved in problem-solving and generating new ideas when he mentioned that his favourite pastime was sitting back in his seat with his feet up on the desk pondering. He said that as much as people wandered past and looked strangely at him, he loved any opportunity he had to really sit back and just think.

Now this doesn't sound all that different to many of us who enjoy the opportunity to flex our creative muscles, but the reason I thought his creative process was unusual was his approach to problem-solving. This CEO loved to be approached with problems, whether by a client, supplier or staff member. Naturally I had to ask why, and his response was that when someone approached him with a problem it gave him a chance to think, and he relished the opportunity to sit down and search about for a solution to a problem. Too often he said he found himself caught up in the day-to-day activities of the business without having an opportunity to think differently, problem-solve, challenge how things might be done or find a new way of doing something.

During your lifetime you are always going to be faced with problems of one sort or another that you cannot control, whether job related or personal. What you can control however is your approach to those same problems, and it is your attitude that really matters. Most people run from problems as they see them as a pain in the rear end and a challenge they could well do without. Stop and think for a moment how you would approach problems if you saw them as being opportunities to flex your creative muscles to find solutions to challenges.

No matter what role you play in your organisation or even whether it is in or out of the workplace, *how* you approach a problem is more important than the actual issue itself or the process involved in solving the problem. As self-help guru Doctor Wayne Dyer says in one of my favourite quotes, 'As you think, so shall you be.' If you see the positive side of problems and issues, then that's how you will approach them, as an opportunity to really think and exercise your creative muscles. You will tend to find better, more productive ideas and solutions when you approach them with a positive attitude, and you will also have a much happier disposition, outcome and approach to the bigger picture — life itself.

So the next time you are faced with a problem, think of it as an opportunity to think. Know in your own mind that you *will* find an answer and it *will* be great. Know that you *can do it*.

Think about that!

A creativity/thinking differently joke

A pastor, a doctor and an engineer were waiting one morning for a particularly slow group of golfers to move on to the next hole on the golf course. The engineer fumed, 'What's with these guys? We must have been waiting for fifteen minutes!' The doctor chimed in, 'I don't know, but I've never seen such ineptitude.'

The pastor said, 'Hey, here comes the greenkeeper. Let's have a word with him.' (Dramatic pause.)

'Hi George. Say, what's with that group ahead of us? They're rather slow, aren't they?'

The greenkeeper replied, 'Oh, yes, that's a group of blind fire-fighters. They lost their sight saving our clubhouse from a fire last year, so we always let them play for free any time.'

The group was silent for a moment.

The pastor said, 'That's so sad. I think I will say a special prayer for them tonight.'

The doctor said, 'Good idea. And I'm going to contact my ophthalmologist buddy and see if there's anything he can do for them.'

The engineer said, 'Why can't they play at night?'

Now that's thinking differently!

ARE YOU TALKING TO ME?

One of the greatest barriers I have observed when facilitating creativity, achievement or planning sessions is self-belief. The word I hear most often in these workshops is 'can't'. The fact is that when we say to ourselves 'we can't', the brain, which cannot distinguish between what is real and what is imaginary, assumes that what we are saying is fact, and then searches for evidence to back it up. Whenever you say you can't do something, you are programming your brain to accept a lesser option. One of the most effective tools that you can harness in order to achieve and get more out of your life is the ability to control that little voice inside your head.

But it is easier said than done. I am very aware of my own little voice, but now and then I really have to give myself a good talking to in order to change the language that I'm hearing in my head. Being a runner, I am very aware of the little voice that kicks in at the back end of a race, telling me that 'it is okay to slow down', or indeed to stop. That is one of the reasons I enjoy marathons so much — it's just you and that constant dialogue in your head. Programming that little voice to tell me to keep on going no matter what can make all the difference at the finish line.

The most effective way of controlling this voice is to eliminate 'can't' from your vocabulary, inside your head and out loud to those around you. As Henry Ford once said: 'If you think you can or think you can't, either way you are right.'

What you think will determine the outcome of whatever endeavour you pursue. Whether it's doing a tricky calculation for a payroll, painting a picture, going that extra mile for a walk or run in the morning, or simply getting out of bed before the sun comes up, it's that little voice inside your head that will either help or hinder you. The same thing applies to those people who say, 'I am trying to lose weight,' or, 'I am trying to give up smoking.' There is no need to tell that little voice inside your head that this is the case.

The voice that chatters away in your head all day programs you to achieve, or to give up and fail. In the early 1950s, the biggest challenge for any track or field runner was to break the four-minute mark for running a mile. It was a goal that no-one was able to reach. It had eluded a number of professional runners for many years. In 1954, Roger Bannister cracked it and ran the mile in less than four minutes. For years, many had tried and many had failed. What is interesting is that once Bannister had done it, no fewer than fifty runners broke the four-minute mile in that same year. What changed? Suddenly people went from 'it's impossible' to 'it's doable'. All that changed for these runners was the language in their mind.

A young Hungarian Jewish boy called John Saunders arrived in Australia many years ago. On arrival he bought a Hebrew-English dictionary. He took a red pen and scribbled out the word 'impossible' so that it never existed in his dictionary or his vocabulary. John Saunders went on to partner another chap called Frank Lowy in developing the biggest shopping centre organisation in the world. Today, many of us shop at Westfield because John Saunders pursued a dream that might have seemed impossible, but was everything but since 'impossible' simply didn't exist in his mindset.

To strive to be the best that you can be, change your language. Take out the words 'can't', 'try' and 'impossible', and enjoy the impact it makes on your life, your goals, your children, your family and your workmates.

WHAT A WASTE OF A DAY ...

As a corporate trainer and facilitator I am constantly amazed at how people waste their time and money at conferences! At corporate conferences all over Australia and overseas, I constantly see attendees wiping themselves out partying until the wee hours of the morning, with no thought as to the impact it has on the overall outcome of the conference. Now I have no problem with people kicking up their heels, letting their hair down and relaxing — sometimes it's good for the creative mind. However, when these same people turn up at the start of the following day bleary-eyed, hung-over, feeling sick with a headache and they are expecting to contribute to a corporate vision or strategy, they are just kidding themselves.

When you go away on a company conference and party, it may not be your money that you're wasting, but it is your time. How anybody can waste a complete day of his or her life through partying to the wee hours is beyond me. On the other hand, there are also a large number of people at these same conferences who go to the dinner, have a few drinks, have great conversation and a few laughs, and then hit the sack at a reasonable hour, ready to embrace the next day. If you're heading off on a conference, don't wipe yourself out and then expect to be able to contribute anything of much value to the group the next day. Sure, there are those who can somehow hit it hard and then back up, but I would question if those people are giving the conference 100% or working to their total capacity.

When you are taken away to a conference at a resort, it's not a day off. It's a day when your company expects you to contribute and assist the company in being the best it can be. If you're turning up any less than the best you can be then you are wasting your time, your day, your company's money and an opportunity to be great. I'd love a dollar for every time somebody has said that the conference is an 'opportunity to communicate better'. Yet these are so often the very same people who are turning up at these conferences, writing themselves off, sitting around bleary-eyed and comatose, until the final whistle at 5.00 or 6.00 o'clock. The people who aren't contributing or communicating so often turn around and say: 'What about communication?'

Consider the difference in outcomes that these two companies would have experienced from their conferences …

I was running a session in the southern states recently and on the first night a group of participants decided to party pretty hard. After karaoke until 3.00 o'clock in the morning, these same people fronted up to the workshop, cans of Coke in hand, looking like they hadn't slept for a week. These people sat there and agonised as the minutes ticked by, until they could return to their room to hit the sack. Did they waste the day? Absolutely. Did they waste some company money? Absolutely. Was it a waste of time them being there? Absolutely.

In contrast, I recently facilitated a fantastic two-day creative session at The Vault. The company involved had spent four years and over $60,000 in the process of bringing their national team together for this event. Since they were all being put up at the same hotel and drinks and dinner were organised for both nights, I was expecting the worst. To my relief, the coordinator for the conference — a fun-loving and well-respected team member — got up at the start of the first day and expressed his wish list. One wish was that everyone would have a great time, come up with some great ideas and get to know each other. Another was that everyone would conserve their energy over the two days. He specifically requested that people 'go easy' on the first night as the second day would be a long but eventful one, and that it would be wasted if the team were trashed. This simple advice, given with warmth and empathy, was well received. They turned up for day two ready to create, contribute and make the best use of their time together, and as a result had a fun and productive day.

In the end, a lot of it is about communication. It's also about your company culture, and letting your team know that their time and input is valued. After all, time is your most precious commodity. Don't waste it!

A MODERN DAY MYTH ...

Earlier in the book I told you about an exercise I do with some groups in my workshops where I have them write an imaginary story about their partner. After the exercise, I always have a lot of people approach me to tell me how much they enjoyed the exercise and that it has been years since they were able to use their imaginations in this way and open their minds up to a world of possibilities. With that in mind, I thought I would give you an easy exercise that you can do yourself, with your children or friends, or perhaps you can use it in a workshop environment with your business, charity or social group. I am often asked for simple exercises that groups can do as an energiser, group-starter, or as a kick-start to a meeting or session, and the Modern Day Myth is a terrific exercise for that purpose. It is a lot of fun, easy to run, and you always get great results.

All you need to do is to print off copies of the following page and hand it to each person in your group. The idea is that each person is to allow their imagination to run free, and they simply fill in the blanks in the story. I have used this particular story for groups of children right through to groups of creative directors of big-name advertising agencies, and it never ceases to amaze me how even such diverse groups manage to get such a kick and a thrill out of doing this exercise. Each time I do it with an individual or a group I also do it myself, and I am always amused at the different ways I end up writing the story.

Remember when starting the exercise to tell people that there are no right or wrong answers, and it is their story so they should write it the way they want to. Ask them not to edit their stories but to just write down on the paper whatever comes to mind first; don't ponder, just read the line and fill in the gaps. They will find it much more fun, more imaginative, and more stimulating to just go with the flow. I usually give my groups about seven minutes to complete the exercise.

Once you have completed the exercise, you can then either have the person doing the writing read it out or have the group read them to each other. If you wish, there are a number of ways you can summarise the exercise around imagination, creativity and the fact that the group needs to access the same imagination they used to write the story to solve the opportunity, question or puzzle confronting you, your children or your social group. It really is a simple yet wonderful exercise to help people open up their imagination and to prove to themselves that their imagination is there, they just have to find the right the keys to unlock it.

A modern day myth

Once upon a time, a very special child called
_____ came into the
world. Unbeknown to his/her family,
_____ was a child of
great _____, and his/her
creator intended for him/her to _____
_____
whilst on earth.

It was not until _____
became older that he/she realised his/her power
to be able to _____
_____ ,
and give _____
to those around him/her.

Unfortunately _____
also discovered there were some people who

_____

his/her special gift, and they began to

_____ .

However, _____
refused to be brought down by these
people, and with never-failing belief,

_____ was able to

_____.

When it came time for _____
to leave this world, he/she looked back on his/
her life and knew that he/she had accomplished

_____ ,

and felt glad.

When _____ returned
to his/her creator, he/she was congratulated on
achieving such success during his/her time in
the world. As the ultimate gift to the world,
he/she left, _____ requested that
_____ and _____
_____

be given to that world in abundance for ever
more, and that wish was granted.

The end

7 FINAL THOUGHTS ...

I really do hope that you have enjoyed *The Keys to Creativity*, and that the content has caused you not only to rethink your perception of your own creativity, but that it has also changed your approach to idea generation on every level, both in and out of the workplace.

The next time someone approaches you to ask for an idea or a solution to a problem, I hope that you feel confident that you have a collection of tools, a 'key ring' full of ideas to access, that will readily give you some different ways and means of coming up with ideas and solutions. The world really is full of mediocrity and of people afraid to think outside the square — your ideas can make you stand out from the crowd in the most positive and rewarding of ways.

If you have children, start to exercise their creative muscles when they are young. Plant the seed of creativity, and nurture it until they grow to an age where they can harvest it and reap the rewards. Our future is in the hands of those who can think differently, so plant the seeds in your children as soon as you possibly can.

IDEAS DON'T WORK UNLESS YOU DO!

Above all else, please remember that *ideas don't work unless you do!* I encourage you to take the final step to unlocking your creative potential by *doing* something with the tips and tools that I have shared with you in the book. Here are a few suggestions to get you started:

Teach someone else

Take a few principles from the book and teach someone else — you will reinforce the ideas and you will be giving yourself a much deeper understanding of the concepts at the same time. Perhaps you could even use a sales meeting or team work-in-progress meeting to share with the group something from the book.

Do a summary of your thoughts on the book

When I finish a book, I always take a few minutes to do a quick, single-page summary of the parts of that book that I found valuable or of particular relevance to me. I find the process of doing this quick summary allows me to take extra value from the books I read, and also allows me to recap and re-learn valuable information that I might otherwise have forgotten. I put each of the summaries I create into a journal set aside just for this purpose. By having these thoughts and ideas, themes and page references recorded in one book, I can find specific material quickly when I wish to access it, and the book becomes my own ultimate personal reference book.

I usually begin my summaries by noting down the name of the book in the centre of the page. From the centre I work gradually outwards, including gradually more and more detailed information. I may begin the process by noting down the themes of chapters from the book that I found interesting. After that I tend to fill the page with favourite quotes, pieces I can use in meetings and workshops, short key words and page numbers that I can refer back to quickly, as well as any other interesting titbits that I believe will be of use to me in future. It will only take ten to fifteen minutes to do your summary, so why not give it a try? Use colour, drawings, doodles and diagrams to give it some fun and dimension.

Remember my suggestion at the very beginning of the book to read with a highlighter nearby, so that you could highlight interesting and valuable quotes, content and phrases? Now that you have finished the book, you can go through and collate all of those highlighted bits and pieces into your summary. This technique also has the added benefit of increasing the retention and recall of the books you read.

Just do it

Take the time to think, apply the Creative Dancea to a project, visualise your next problem, use the BiGNOA instead of the traditional SWOT on your business ... just make use of the tools and try them out yourself! The reason 'Just do it' was so successful for Nike was due to the fact that most people 'don't do it'. They make all sorts of excuses, get distracted, blame others or just can't be bothered. These same people then go and buy a pair of Nike shoes, shorts or a t-shirt to make themselves feel like they 'did it'. There is great power in making a start.

Set yourself some written goals

It is amazing how goals, once written down, can come to fruition. It has been said that a goal not written down is just a dream without a deadline. I constantly find myself in situations where I have been able to achieve my goals, and I can honestly say that I am not always sure how they came about. One thing I do know, however, is that it seems to happen the most when those goals are in writing!

Practise

Creativity is like a muscle; the more you use it, the more it grows. To borrow a line from the Hollywood block-buster film *The Matrix*, 'I can show you the door, you're the one who's got to walk through it.' Actually, I can even give you the keys to the door, but you are still the one who has to use the keys to open the door to your own creativity. Work your creative muscles and they will grow.

I once read a book by Wayne Bennett, the coach of an Australian rugby team called the Brisbane Broncos, entitled *Don't Die with the Music In You*. I can't think of a better title to sum up my views on creativity. Please don't die with the ideas in you — understand your ability, trust your innate talent, have courage, be persistent, have some fun, play ... and let your ideas grow to see the light of day! Each and every day somewhere in the world, a great idea will not see the light of day because a person did not speak up — please don't let that happen to you. Take the keys and drive your ideas and your own destiny. It's your creative vehicle, so take it for a spin.

I have mentioned in the book that I am a big fan of Robin Williams. I will leave you with a line from one of his movies, *Jack*. At the end of the movie, during his graduation speech, the character looks out into the sea of young faces and says to his fellow classmates, *'Make your life spectacular.'* This is your chance; it is your world, your time ... and your decision, to not just have a good life, or a good time, but to use your imagination and *'make your life spectacular'*. Why can't this be *you*! Make that life your own!

Think about it!

Appendix A:
Gary's recommended book list

Creativity

Jump Start Your Brain, Doug Hall

101 Creative Problem Solving Techniques,
    James M Higgins

Cross-Train Your Brain, Stephen D Eiffert

Train Your Brain, Dr Harry Adler

The Art of Possibility, Rosamund and Benjamin Zander

The Solutions Focus,
    Paul Z Jackson and Mark McKergow

The Power of Full Engagement, Jim Loehr

Marketing

The 22 Immutable Laws of Branding, Al and Laura Ries

What Were They Thinking?, Robert McMath

Jump Start Your Business Brain, Doug Hall

The Art of War, Sun Tzu

Differentiate or Die, Jack Trout

A New Brand World, Scott Bedbury

Effective communication

How to Give It so They Get It, Sharon Bowman

NLP in 21 days, Harry Adler and Beryl Heather

Selling with NLP, Kerry Johnson

Training with NLP,
   Joseph O'Connor and John Seymour

Slowing Down to the Speed of Life,
   Richard Carlson and Joseph Bailey

The Good Listener, Hugh MacKay

APPENDIX B:
BLUE MOON WORKSHOP
CD RECOMMENDATIONS

Workshop groove
(music for breakouts)

Café Del Mar — Volumen Ocho, Various artists

Logical Progression — Level 1, LTJ Buken

Logical Progression — Level 1 CD3: Classics, LTJ Buken

Tierra De Nadie, Hevia

Verve Remixed, Various artists

Workshop relax
(music for thinking)

Day Dreams, Various artists

Echoes of the Upper Missouri, Keith Bear

Garden of Serenity, David Gordon

John Williams Plays the Movies, John Williams

Shepherd Moons, Enya

The Memory of Trees, Enya

Heart of the World, Mary Youngblood

White Buffalo, Robert Tree Cody and Rob Wallace

Dreams from the Grandfather, Robert Tree Cody

Canyon Trilogy, Robert Tree Cody

The Mozart Effect, Music for Children,
   Volume 1: Tune Up Your Mind,
      Wolfgang Amadeus Mozart (Composer), et al

Music for the Mozart Effect, Volume 3:
   Unlock the Creative Spirit,
      Wolfgang Amadeus Mozart, (Composer), et al

Even Wolves Dream, Anthony Miles

APPENDIX C:
GUIDED VISUALISATION

Begin by finding a comfortable place to lie or sit. Loosen any tight clothing and remove your shoes. This is your time to relax. There is nowhere to go and nothing to do.

With your eyes closed, focus all of your attention on your breathing. Let your tummy rise and fall with each breath. Breathe in, breathe out. Breathe in, breathe out, and as you exhale, slowly repeat the word in your mind 'relax'. Say it softly and slowly as you feel any tension drain out of your body.

Continue to breathe slowly, repeating the word 'relax' with every outward breath. Think about your feet and relax your feet. Now focus on your legs, and relax your legs. Now think about your back — take all that stress and just relax. Now think about your stomach; breathe in, breathe out and just relax.

In your mind's eye, imagine that you are standing on a cliff overlooking a beautiful beach and the ocean below. The beach seems to stretch on forever. You can hear the waves as they crash, and the fresh sea breeze. Directly in front of you is an elevator — it may be made out of shiny steel, maybe bamboo or glass, even cotton wool, or perhaps you are stepping onto a cloud. Whatever you see, step into your elevator and we're going to go down from five to one, and with every floor as we go down, we're going to become more and more relaxed. Going down from five to four, feel your body become lighter, feel the relaxation and tranquillity flowing through your whole body. Three — feel the letting go. Go deeper and deeper as you become more relaxed. Two — all the tension completely drains away. One — completely relax now, completely let go. Go deeper and deeper.

Totally relaxed, and now walking out onto the beach, feel and see the soft sand sparkling like tiny diamonds beneath your feet. Feel the sun radiating like warm diamonds beneath your feet. Feel the sun radiating down warm on your face and on your body. You can feel the sun, you can smell the sea breeze, and you notice how beautifully blue the sky is as you hear the small waves crashing on the shoreline.

As you walk towards the water you notice a little further up the beach a large hot-air balloon with all the colours of the rainbow in its canopy. So you start to walk towards the balloon, making your way along the beach, and when you get close, you notice that hanging underneath the canopy is a basket. And as you get even closer, you can read a sign on the basket that says, 'Throw in any worries, any pains, any aches, any problems you have, just throw them in the basket.'

Now take a few moments to go through your body and mind like a large tea strainer and just throw any problems you have in the basket. Anything that's worrying you, anything that's occupying your mind — throw it in the basket. As you stand there at the water's edge, feeling light and free, the balloon begins to drift away. You watch it as it floats further and further into the sky, floating away until it becomes just a small speck in the distance. And finally, the balloon disappears. Enjoy that feeling now and know that this is your place. And that you can come here whenever you like and make your way along the beach to your balloon, and drop in your worries.

Making your way back up the beach, you step towards your elevator. Stepping in, and with every floor, as you go up, you are becoming more and more aware of your body. Level one — bring your awareness back to your breathing. Two — just wiggle your toes and your fingertips. Three — move your feet, your legs, and your arms. Level four — let your head roll from side to side and move your body slowly. As we get back up to the top of the cliff and to level five, you are back in the room now feeling refreshed and totally rejuvenated. In your own time, slowly open your eyes, and when you are ready, sit up.

Appendix D: Mum's meringue recipe

Ingredients:

1 egg white

1 teaspoon vinegar

1 cup caster sugar

2 tablespoons hot water

1 teaspoon vanilla essence

1 teaspoon baking powder

Method:

Beat all ingredients except baking powder together until creamy and stiff.

Fold a small teaspoon of baking powder into the mixture.

Pipe shapes onto lightly greased baking tray.

Bake in a slow oven for about 1 hour.

(Makes a dozen meringues, depending on how large you make them.)

Enjoy!

INDEX

ABOUT THE AUTHOR

Gary Bertwistle has been working in the area of creativity for twenty years, starting in the retail industry with department stores and retail shopping centres, before moving into the highly creative music industry, managing and promoting bands and artists.

He was appointed Group General Manager of Promotions and Marketing for Austereo Pty Ltd, Australia's largest radio network, overseeing the marketing and promotions of thirteen radio stations on the 2Day and Triple M Networks in Australia, and five stations in Kuala Lumpur. In this role he created ideas for some of Australia's best known brands.

Gary is Australia's newest pioneer in Creative Thinking. His presentations change the way people think, problem-solve and create. His training company — Blue Moon Creative — assists organisations in unlocking their great ideas.

Gary's creative endeavours have resulted in the innovation and creation of Blue Moon Creative's exclusive 'Mind Tools' — The Spider Web, BiGNOA, The Spin Cycle and Ask Einstein. These tools have been developed to assist companies

and teams brainstorm more effectively, unlock their ideas and put their great ideas into action.

He has also designed and built The Vault, Australia's first ever dedicated creative space, designed specifically for the generation of better ideas. The Vault's octagonal shape, natural light, outdoor space, furniture and facilities make it a unique and exciting venue for workshops or meetings.

BLUE MOON CREATIVE

All the creative tools referred to in
this book are available on our website.
For these and for more information
regarding Blue Moon Creative, The Vault,
or any of our workshops, please visit
www.bluemooncreative.com.au.

To have Gary speak at your
next conference or team session,
please contact Gary:
gary@bluemoon.net.au.

Or call Blue Moon Creative's office on
(02) 9356 4788.